[redacted]

Asians in the West

Also by Edwin P. Hoyt

Alexander Woollcott: The Man Who Came to Dinner
American Attitude: The Story of the Making of Foreign Policy in the United States
Andrew Johnson
The Carrier War
Count von Luckner: Knight of the Sea
Deadly Craft: Fire Ships to PT Boats
Destroyers: Foxes of the Sea
Franklin Pierce: The Fourteenth President of the United States
From the *Turtle* to the *Nautilus*: The Story of Submarines
Germans Who Never Lost: The Story of the *Königsberg*
Ghost Lane
The Glorious Flattops
Guggenheims and the American Dream
He Freed the Minds of Men: René Descartes
How They Won the War in the Pacific: Nimitz and His Admirals
James Buchanan
James Knox Polk
John Quincy Adams
John Tyler
Leland Stanford
Leyte Gulf: The Death of the *Princeton*
Marilyn: The Tragic Venus
Martin Van Buren
The Nixons: An American Family
Palmer Raids, 1919–1920: An Attempt to Suppress Dissent
Phantom Raider
Space Dealers
William McKinley
Your Health Insurance: A Story of Failure
Zachary Taylor
Zeppelins

ASIANS IN THE WEST

by Edwin P. Hoyt

publishers since 1798

THOMAS NELSON INC., PUBLISHERS

Nashville New York

 Published in Nashville, Tennessee, by Thomas Nelson Inc., and simultaneously in Don Mills, Ontario, by Thomas Nelson & Sons (Canada) Limited. Manufactured in the United States of America.

First edition

Library of Congress Cataloging in Publication Data

Hoyt, Edwin Palmer.
Asians in the West.

Bibliography: p.
1. Asians in the United States—History. 2. United States—Emigration and immigration—History. I. Title.
E184.06H66 917.3'06'95 74-10269
ISBN 0-8407-6399-9

Contents

Asians in the West

Chapter One

The West Beckons Asia

In the middle of the nineteenth century, the United States and Europe were deeply involved in the period of economic growth known as the Industrial Revolution. From this economic growth came renewed Western expansion all over the undeveloped world and the height of the imperialistic period of history. In a nutshell, that is why the emigration of Asians from their homelands to the West developed as it did, bringing heartbreak, tragedy, and disgrace to the Western world that is matched only by the treatment of the blacks.

The Indians of North and South America were exploited, exterminated, and mistreated by Caucasians. So were the peoples of Africa and the blacks, Melanesians, and Polynesians of the Pacific. But in the story of Asians in the West, there is high adventure, tragedy, and promise of a different kind.

Beginning in the sixteenth century, Europeans made slaves of the blacks and the native peoples of the Western Hemisphere. Many of these peoples came from Stone Age societies. Certain black societies of Africa were more advanced, however, and the Inca, Aztec, and Maya of the Western world had real civilizations. Their people were adept at mathematics, astronomy, and agriculture as well as the arts.

The situation with Asia and the Asians was different. When the real opening of Asia to the West began in the middle of the nineteenth century, the Asians already had sophisticated societies, which they felt were superior to those of the Western world.

China, Japan, India, and the region known as Indochina were to have the greatest impact on the West because they were to send the most people abroad. All of these lands were highly civilized in the middle of the nineteenth century. Considering them by Western terms, one might even say they were well past their prime and rotting in decadence. Politically and militarily, these societies were weak as compared to the Western powers, and that is another reason why the history of Asians in the West developed as it did.

Portuguese, Spanish, and Italian missionaries and traders went to China in the fifteenth and sixteenth centuries, when China was strong. The British went in the early years of the nineteenth century and were followed by other Western powers, whose main interest at the time was trade. American influence in China began in the 1830's, when the missionaries went to South China. This is significant, because the vast majority of the hundreds of thousands of Chinese who emigrated to America were to come from this area, largely from three districts around Canton in Kwangtung Province.

To a very large extent, the immigration of all Asians to the Western world was the result of poverty and misery in their homelands in the nineteenth century. Nowhere is this better shown than in the story of Chinese migration to America, which was far more significant than Chinese movement to any other part of the Western world.

In 1844 the United States and the Manchu emperor of China concluded the Treaty of Wanghsia, which opened China to American traders on a large scale. At first most of this trade was conducted in the Canton area.

Nationalist-minded Chinese, many of whom were exposed to the religious teachings of Protestant missionaries, became restless under the special, almost godlike treatment given foreigners in their land. From this unrest came the T'ai P'ing Rebellion against the Manchu rulers. The rebellion began in 1850 and lasted fourteen years. Much of the revolutionary activity occurred in the north, but South China suffered too. At the same time as the T'ai P'ing Rebellion, Americans had begun to develop California, and the gold rush there beckoned the poor villagers of South China, just as they were being threatened by famine, plundering warlords, and the social unrest of a dying empire.

During this period shrewd Chinese traders, operating from Canton and Hong Kong, began to fan out all around the world, and they established Chinese colonies almost everywhere. How astute the Chinese were as businessmen was shown by the way these men emerged and adapted themselves. By the beginning of the twentieth century, Chinese bankers and merchants controlled much of the business of Southeast Asia and the Pacific area. Wherever the Europeans went and took power, the Chinese followed and established trading posts. Indochina, Malaya, the Dutch East Indies, the Philippines, and the Pacific Islands all beckoned the Chinese.

But the gold of California beckoned the poor. Around 1850 the Chinese practice was for a family to send one or more of its unmarried sons out into the world to earn his fortune. From overseas he was expected to send money home. Eventually, he was expected to return home, either to acquire a wife, take her back to the new land, and continue to send money to his parents, or to settle down at home, if his fortune was large enough. This was the family social system, and it persisted throughout the important days of Chinese immigration into the United States.

At first, when the news of the big discovery at Sutter's Mill was still reverberating throughout America, the Chinese were treated well enough. The Kwangtung peasants were hardworking, and they gladly undertook the tasks that Caucasian Americans found distasteful. They settled down to provide the basic services of the gold camps and of the towns, such as San Francisco, that sprang up to provide for the camps. Chinese cooks, laundrymen, and storekeepers settled in. Chinese laborers and dishwashers were accepted. So were a few Chinese merchants.

But soon these ambitious, hardworking Chinese learned that they too could go into the goldfields and search for the real wealth. Thus, although in 1850 the San Francisco newspaper *Alta Californian* was warm in its praise of these "very useful, quiet, good citizens"—the Chinese—two years later hostility began. Part of the reason was the increase in Chinese immigration as the word got back to the Canton area that men could become rich in America. Twenty thousand Chinese came to California in 1852, and most of them were headed for the goldfields.

The Anglo-Saxon Caucasians had already been successful in pushing Mexicans, Chileans, Frenchmen, and other "foreigners" out of the mining camps. Their most effective weapon was the new state's legislature, which in 1850 imposed an exorbitant monthly tax on all miners who were not native-born Americans. The Mexicans and all the others left the mining camps very quickly, and the tax was dropped.

Then came the Chinese—and violence. The winter of 1852 saw a rash of beatings, murders, robberies, and even hangings of Chinese, simply because they wanted to mine alongside the Caucasians. In El Dorado County the miners stopped the Chinese from coming in at all. Throughout the mining district, the Chinese were harried and burned out if they did not leave. In 1853 only four thousand Chinese came to California from Kwangtung.

For the next ten years those brave Chinese who continued to mine did so under constant threats of violence and were forced to pay exorbitant taxes imposed by the state and the counties. The common folk stories were full of tales of the "heathen Chinee," and there was a joke in the camps that if a miner ran out of money, all he had to do was wait for a Chinese to come along and rob him.

Even though the Chinese were unpopular because they took jobs that Caucasians thought should be their own, the Chinese aroused a grudging respect for their clean habits, honesty, and hard work. Very seldom did a Chinese appear in court accused of a real crime. The crimes were committed against them, not by them.

Then came the building of the transcontinental railway, and the situation of the Chinese in America changed once again. Their renewed "opportunity," if it can be called that, came when Collis P. Huntington, Charles Crocker, and Leland Stanford started building the Central Pacific Railroad, which was to connect with the Union Pacific somewhere east of the Sierra Nevada.

The Eastern railroads were built by European immigrants, many of them Irish. Early in the 1860's Crocker arranged for advertising in newspapers in Ireland, and thousands of young men applied to come to America to escape the depression in their homeland. In California, however, the diversions and the climate were such that at the end of two years the Central Pacific was getting nowhere. Only fifty miles of track had been laid, and the worst was yet to come. The Irish lost their enthusiasm for the job. There were too many easier ways to make a living. In 1865 Crocker advertised for five thousand workers and secured fewer than one thousand.

Facing failure, Crocker decided to go against public pressure and hire Chinese laborers. First he hired fifty men to fill dump wagons. They did it so well that they were put to work with picks. In six months there were three thousand Chinese on the Central Pacific payroll, and the work was moving ahead. Soon there were thousands more. At the height of construction, nine out of ten workers on the railroad were Chinese.

The Chincse put the line through the stormy Sierra Nevada, working in the winter in snow so deep that they had to burrow their way out of their camps. The light of day never penetrated into their snowbound huts in winter. Lowered in baskets from the cliff, Chinese blasters put the road across the almost perpendicular face of the mountain called Cape Horn. They tamped in explosives, lighted fuses, and pulled themselves up hand over hand, hoping to escape the blasts. Not all did. The bones of hundreds of Chinese were left in the rocks of the Sierras in those winters.

Because of the Chinese laborers, and only because of them, Crocker, Huntington, and Stanford were able to finish their railroad. In 1869 the golden spike that connected the Central Pacific and the Union Pacific was driven in at Promontory Point, Utah. There were many speeches, toasts, and champagne. There was not one word of praise for the Chinese who had built the railroad.

Because of the need for railroad labor, life in 1868 seemed to look brighter for the poor Chinese peasants who had come to seek their fortune in California. The Burlingame Treaty of that year established the "inalienable right" of men to travel freely from one country to another "for the purpose of curiosity, of trade, or as permanent residents." It also established the "principle" of reciprocal privileges for Chinese traveling in America and Americans traveling in China. If that treaty was to be followed, the Chinese would have no more trouble.

During the last years of the 1860's and the early years of the 1870's, all went fairly well. The Chinese were still resented because they worked too hard or were too frugal and because they were Orientals; but rail lines had to be built to connect the growing cities with the main lines, and the Chinese built them. Orchards and farms had to be tended, and the Chinese went willingly to do work they knew well from the old country, where most of them were farmers.

The story of Japanese immigration and settlement in the United States is different only in detail. The reason for large-scale immigration of Japanese was the same—a group of Caucasian capitalists needed cheap labor and therefore encouraged Japanese immigration. When the need had ended and the Japanese tried to better themselves, they became an economic threat to some Caucasians and thus the enemy.

Japanese immigration was really the idea of the Americans, not of the Japanese rulers. For some four hundred years the emperors and the shoguns of Japan had outlawed emigration from the islands. They resisted contact with the Western world until 1853, when Commodore Matthew Perry forced his way into Japan and threatened the imperial state with violence, so that the rulers were cowed into accepting a relationship they hated. In the 1850's some fifteen hundred Japanese, of the upper class for the most part, came to America to learn the language and the customs. Then a few students, merchants, traders, and even settlers began to come in.

Among the first Japanese colonies was one established near Sacramento by a German named Eduard Schnell. He was married to a wealthy Japanese girl, and he had a dream of bringing the fruits of Japanese culture to America. At the risk of the lives of all of them, he smuggled a group of artisans and artists out of the Japanese islands to take up the new life at Gold Hill, California. Their dream was to grow bamboo and mulberry trees, make silk, grow tea, and produce the things indigenous to Japan, but the colony did not prosper and was soon forgotten.

The real impetus for Japanese immigration came with the development of the sugar and pineapple plantations in Hawaii. Because of the settlement first of missionaries and then of businessmen from America, Hawaii had a special economic relationship with the United States long before Sanford B. Dole and a gang of other Americans overthrew the Hawaiian monarchy in 1894. Even before 1868 the Americans dominated the economic life of the islands. That was the year in which they secured from a reluctant Japanese government the right to recruit contract laborers in Japan for transportation to the cane and pineapple fields. This contact with the West came at a time when the Japanese population was expanding rapidly, and so ten years later the Emperor relaxed the restrictions against emigration. After that there was a steady flow of Japanese workers to the Hawaiian Islands, which mounted into the thousands in the 1880's.

When Hawaii was annexed to the United States, the Japanese residents of the Islands gained the right to come to the mainland without passports. So they began moving to the West Coast. At the same time other Japanese went to British Columbia, while some established colonies on the west coast of South America. All this was going on even as the uproar broke out in the United States against the Chinese.

The Japanese immigrants to America, those who were born in Japan, were called the *Issei* in Japanese. They, like the Chinese, were largely farmers. They worked hard, saved their money, and did not ask for charity. They took lands that were substandard, such as those of the Sacramento delta, and made them bloom. Some, like George Shima, became millionaires.

Shima came to the United States in 1890 as a labor contractor, supplying workers to Caucasian farmers in California. He saved his money and bought a little land in the San Joaquin River Valley near Stockton. This region was called the tule region because of the worthless vegetation by that name that covered it. The river flooded the area in the winter and made it apparently useless, but George Shima knew something about such lands from his life in Japan. He built a dike around one little island and drained the water off into a ditch he cut across the middle. He pumped the water out of the ditch into the river and plowed the land when it dried out. He then let it lie so that the tule and the other vegetation would rot under the turned sod. Finally, he began planting potatoes there.

To help him, Shima brought in relatives from Japan. Soon dozens of people from his villages near Fukuoka in Kyushu had come to the United States to settle and work on the land. They reclaimed one island after another, as the Dutch had reclaimed their lowlands in Holland. They also planted celery and onions, and the farms prospered. Before too long George Shima owned steamboats, barges, and a tugboat line.

But as George Shima and other Japanese prospered in America, they aroused the envy and resentment of some Caucasians. Thus when Shima bought a mansion in Berkeley, which his wealth certainly entitled him to do, there was an outcry from the other residents, who claimed he was spoiling the neighborhood. He put up a huge wall to keep the family apart from the community. He was rich enough to fight off his detractors.

Not all Japanese, by far, became as prosperous as Shima, but most did share his ability to work hard and save money; and their neighbors, watching, grew more envious each year. However, the problem was not too great in the last years of the nineteenth century, as far as the Japanese were concerned. Caucasian resentment was leveled more against the much larger Chinese population, for there were hundreds of thousands of Chinese in the United States and only some twenty-five thousand Japanese. But as the Japanese figure rose and the Chinese declined, because of the pressure on the Chinese to leave the country, resentment increased against the people from Nippon. By 1910, when there were seventy thousand Japanese in the United States, the population was large enough to arouse serious resentment. That is when the troubles of the Japanese in America really began.

Elsewhere in Asia the story was much the same, although the results were not always so immediate or obvious. At the beginning of the nineteenth century, most of what we now call the Indochina area (North and South Vietnam, Cambodia, Laos) was ruled by the emperor of Annam. A succession of emperors kept foreigners from the West from securing any bases in the country, but in 1859 Western imperialism triumphed. French Admiral Rigoult de Genouilly led an expedition that occupied Saigon. Within thirty years the French had taken over the whole area. Thus French suzerainty and French influence over this section of Asia was secured, and the Annamese, as most of the people were known, began to drift toward France when they craved the offerings of Western culture. Colonies of people from the five little states of the Indochina "protectorate" were established in Paris, Marseilles, and other French cities. They brought to France a fine appreciation of Oriental art. They took from France the language, medical knowledge, and some of the skills of modern society, such as engineering, although French restrictions were such that few of these Orientals could go to France, learn such Western specialties, and go home to prosper. The economic stranglehold of colonialism was almost complete.

In spite of this, there was almost no prejudice against Orientals in France itself. There simply were not enough Annamese, Chinese, or other Orientals to become an economic menace at home, and that situation has existed right up to the present day.

The pattern of Asian migration to the British Empire had overtones of both the way of America and the way of France. During the end of the eighteenth and in the nineteenth century, the British Empire was expanding rapidly all over the world. Britain took over Singapore, Malaya, Burma, and other areas. She moved in great strength to consolidate her power in India. With these changes came cultural interchange, resulting from Englishmen living abroad and sometimes marrying Asians, and the welcoming to England of some special groups of the subject peoples, who wanted to learn English ways. Out of this developed such special programs of the Empire as the Rhodes scholarships, offered by the empire builder Cecil Rhodes. These scholarships were prorated for every area of the Empire and even for the United States. Students were invited to England to study at the universities with moneys from Cecil Rhodes' fortune, the idea being that this interchange would bring all parts of the world closer together.

Such scholarships and programs did bring Malays, Burmese, Indians, Pathans, and other peoples to Britain. They contributed color and brought some cultural changes to Britain, particularly in food and eating habits. Tea, of course, had become a British staple long before the Empire gained control of a good share of the tea-producing areas of the world. Indian art, fashions, and scents became popular in Britain. Indian rajas and lesser nobles moved easily in British upper-class society, as did wealthy Chinese from Hong Kong, Malay princes, and rich Singapore merchants. All through the nineteenth and half of the twentieth century, Britain was almost free from any prejudice against Orientals, and she prospered culturally as well as materially from their presence.

But there was another kind of interchange. In 1860 British planters in the southern half of Africa felt the same pinches that the American railroad builders and the Hawaiian sugar planters knew, and they looked around for a source of cheap labor. They found it in India, where famine and poverty were common, and they began bringing large numbers of Indian laborers into the South African states to work the fields.

Britain's liberal policies regarding the interchange of people under the flag of the Empire also brought Indians to Africa. The distance between India and Africa was not large; the opportunity seemed great—at least greater than in the poverty lands of home—and the emergence of Indian colonies encouraged Indian merchants, businessmen, and professionals to go to Africa to work. So by the end of the nineteenth century, there was a very large settlement of Indians in British Africa.

The blacks did not like the Indians, because they took away the middle jobs, leaving only the dregs to the blacks, but the whites did not mind the Indians in the beginning, because they offered no threat. The first signs of repression of the Indians in South Africa began at about the same time that anti-Asian feeling rose to a crescendo in the United States.

Early in the twentieth century, an attempt was made to bring Chinese coolies in to work the South African mines, and some fifty thousand were imported within a matter of months. With so many arriving in such a short time, the reaction was almost immediate, and the Chinese experiment failed. Agitation grew so strong that importation was stopped, and many of those who came in were sent home.

These then were the major Oriental surges to the West, and they brought about a strong reaction, which was to color relations between East and West almost to the present day.

Chapter Two

The Height of Prejudice

In the 1850's, as the Chinese took over San Francisco's Pacific, Jackson, Dupont, and Sacramento streets, the feeling against them grew. The newcomers usually moved into such establishments as the Globe Hotel, on the northwest corner of Jackson and Dupont. In this five-story building with a hundred-foot front, lived 275 Chinese. The street level was occupied by stores. The upper stories were half factory, where shirt collars were made, and half dormitory. The dormitory rooms were perhaps twelve by fourteen feet in area and about fifteen feet high, and were stacked with double bunks. This crowding offended the police department and the fire department.

Virtually none of the Chinese spoke English. Abram Altmeyer, partner in Einstein Brothers Shoe Manufacturing Company, employed 375 "Chinamen" as contract laborers from the Yu Chuy Lung Company, paying them a dollar a day for ten hours' work each day. There was always difficulty in the shop because only one of the Chinese workers spoke English. Most of the Chinese were miserable, and the women were the most miserable of all.

The ministers of the good city were offended by the Chinese prostitutes and greatly exaggerated their number. Yet it was true that in a land without many women, the prostitutes were many. A police officer estimated that of the twelve thousand Chinese women in Chinatown, at least a thousand were prostitutes, living in some fifty houses on Stout's Alley, Spofford Alley, and Sullivan's Alley.

Loi Yau was one of them. This slender young girl was sold by her family in China to the woman brothel keeper Sep Sam, who kept a house in Sullivan's Alley. Loi Yau arrived in San Francisco owing Sep Sam $503 for passage, the money having been paid to her family back in China. Loi Yau contracted to serve Sep Sam as a prostitute for 4½ years in order to pay off the debt. If she ran away during that time and Sep Sam had to send men to catch her, the debt was increased by the amount it cost to find her. If she became ill and was sick for fifteen days, she had to make up a month of extra time. If Sep Sam quit and went back to China, she could sell Loi Yau's contract to another brothel keeper.

Loi Yau's chances of living 4½ years as a prostitute without contracting venereal diease were not very good. Her chances of ever having a normal life, in America or China, were even worse. She became a creature of the damned. Neither missionaries nor authorities knew or cared what happened to old prostitutes.

Much better were the chances of young men who sought to acclimate themselves in Chinatown. Lem Shum came to California in the 1850's, when he was fifteen years old. He was sent out from his little village 150 miles from Canton to serve the family and send home money. He began as a contract worker, but when his father came to America, he lived with his father and had a chance to study English in a mission school in Oakland. His father had been a mining engineer in China, but in California he was just another pig-tailed "heathen Chinee."

Lem Shum went to work in the Christian Mission on Jackson Street. He then began to crusade against Chinese immigration, because he saw the mistreatment of his countrymen in this land.

All through the 1860's two forces were at work against one another in connection with the immigration and residence of the Chinese and other Orientals in America. First was the realization, not untinged with greed, that the Chinese could be used to reclaim land and do work that Occidentals detested. Second was the fear that the Chinese would drive the Occidental Anglo-Saxons out of the lands they had wrested from the Indians and the Mexicans.

During the 1850's and 1860's small groups of Chinese moved to other parts of the United States. At the end of the Civil War some Southerners tried to bring groups of Chinese into the South to speed the industrialization of that section of the country. In July, 1869, planters along the Arkansas River formed a company to bring in Chinese laborers to work their fields. Captain George W. Gift went to Canton with letters of credit, authorized to hire a thousand Chinese laborers. A few weeks later two hundred delegates from Southern states met in the Memphis Opera House to plan for large-scale Chinese immigration to the South, but after the initial enthusiasm the project died out. The South was already facing the very real problem of absorbing some four million former slaves into a wrecked economy.

However, the movement left a few thousand Chinese in the cane fields of Louisiana and on the plantations of Arkansas and Mississippi. The Chinese scattered to Georgia, and many moved to the cities. The trading house of Fou Loy and Company of New Orleans and San Francisco had contracted to bring fifteen hundred laborers from China at twenty-two dollars a month, but once in America, these Chinese soon broke their contracts and headed for the cities.

Chinese were brought to some communities as strikebreakers in the Western states and in the East. At North Adams, Massachusetts, factory owner Calvin T. Sampson brought in two boxcars of Chinese from California in the spring of 1870 to operate his Model Shoe Factory when the workers walked out. The Chinese were to receive twenty-three dollars a month for the first year and twenty-six dollars a month thereafter. This economic threat to the Irish and Italian workers quickly aroused tremendous passion in the East. Wendell Phillips, the abolitionist who had stood for the rights of the enslaved Negroes, came out against the rights of the Chinese and demanded their removal.

Chin Hsien-sheng came to America from the Canton area during this period. He had a job in a hemp factory. Rather, he had been hired in China as a contract worker for the hemp factory, and the job was very much like slave labor. He also peddled vegetables on the side. In those days he used the old Chinese method of peddling, carrying two baskets that hung from a long, supple stick slung across one shoulder. He walked up and down the streets of Boston's Chinatown, singing out his wares in Cantonese.

Chin lived the frugal, hard life of the Chinatown bachelor. He lived in a hotel, slept in a bunk, and ate in cheap restaurants. His lot improved as he gained skills. He learned tailoring and found a market in the red-light district. The Chinese prostitutes liked to wear gay *cheongsams,* or slit dresses, and he could design and sew them. Soon Chin had a flourishing tailoring business and was employing others to do the work while he went out and sold his goods to the ladies of the evening.

Unlike most of his friends, he learned to speak English well and could mix with the Caucasian community. Still, Chin was an exception. As a businessman, he was no threat to the people who hated the Chinese—the Caucasian laboring class.

"Down with the Chinese" read the newspaper headlines. "The Chinese Must Go" became the slogan of that part of the press that had suddenly discovered "the yellow peril."

Feeling had been running high in the West for several years, and the 1870's gave birth to renewed demands for restrictive legislation against Orientals, particularly the Chinese. Almost from the beginning the Chinese had been the subject of a considerable amount of restrictive legislation. In 1854 they had been defined as nonwhite people before the law, the same as American Indians. They could not testify in court and were denied many other rights. In 1859 the California superintendent of education asked that state funds be denied to schools that educated Chinese students.

By the 1870's the Chinese male population of California was nearly fifty-nine thousand, or about 14 percent of the work force. The Chinese dominated the shoe industry of the West, the cigar-making industry, the rope industry. With the outcry against the Chinese in the San Francisco *Times* and the San Francisco *Chronicle,* the violence grew worse. In 1871 it was so serious that the incoming governor mentioned the problem in his inaugural address.

The financial panic of 1873 paralyzed the Eastern industrial Establishment and sent thousands of white workers flocking West for opportunity. Instead of a new start, they came to find themselves standing in long lines while Chinese were working.

Then came years of depression. White workers were discharged in favor of Chinese, who would work harder and for less money. As far as the average American was concerned, that became the crux of the problem.

By the spring of 1876, California's economy had suffered so badly from depression that the movement against the

Chinese found new supporters. The mayor of San Francisco appointed a committee to start a movement against Chinese immigration. The state legislature began a sensational investigation of "crime" and "immorality" among the Chinese. Crowds of thousands gathered to hear denunciations of the Chinese, and tension became so great that the Six Companies, the Chinese merchants of San Francisco, asked for extra police protection. The Pioneer and Mission woolen mills were assigned a hundred extra policemen to protect the Chinese workers from the mobs.

The year 1877 was even worse, because the mining income of the state had declined drastically and brought new financial troubles. The Chinese were blamed for it all, and the intimidation of Chinese workers grew worse. On the night of July 24, 1877, a mob ran amok in San Francisco and attacked all the Chinese they could find. They burned several laundries. They invaded the Chinese section of the city and attacked and mauled both men and women. The governor called out the national guard to protect the Chinese; but the next day the riots continued, and six more stores were destroyed. That afternoon a mob of five hundred men crowded down to the wharves and set fire to the docks of the Pacific Mail Steamship Company, which brought Chinese workers to America. It took three days to restore order.

The violence spread outside San Francisco. In Grass Valley Chinese workers were burned out, and they were also driven out of Colusa and other towns. In Chico five Chinese tenant farmers were murdered and their bodies and cabins burned.

In 1878 and 1879 the harassment grew. In the latter year the delegates to the state constitutional convention put in an anti-Chinese article that forbade the employment of Chinese by corporations and gave the legislature full power to regulate the immigration of all persons. The article was passed. That same year California's Senator Booth in Washington proposed the first national anti-Chinese immigration bill. By this time feeling had been aroused North and South, East and West, and the bill passed both houses of Congress. However, it was vetoed in 1880 by President Rutherford Hayes because the Burlingame Treaty was a higher law that could not be thus contravened.

Still the pressure grew in California. Hundreds of workers marched against plants that employed Chinese and demanded their discharge. Some industries closed down entirely because of the harassment. The legislature passed more restrictive legislation, this time outlawing the employment of Chinese by corporations.

One after another, these laws were declared unconstitutional, but the emotions that caused them were not stilled. The agitation for anti-Chinese immigration laws continued. The Democratic party backed such a disgraceful program, partly because of its commitment to the cause of organized labor, partly because the Southern Democrats saw the Chinese problem in the West as being similar to the black problem in the South. So racism triumphed in 1882, and the result was the Chinese Exclusion Act—one of the most disgraceful pieces of legislation ever offered Congress and a lasting blot on the record of the Democratic party, because without almost solid Democratic support, the Western hysteria would certainly have failed.

This act banned the immigration of "Chinese laborers," which meant all Chinese, skilled and unskilled, who might wise to work in the United States. It also denied the right of future citizenship to any Chinese, a right they had not had under the Burlingame Treaty either. The purpose was not only to stop Chinese immigration, but to drive the existing Chinese out of the country. On May 6, 1882, Congress passed this law. President Chester Arthur signed it, and it went into effect. The only voices heard loudly above the clamor were those of a handful of New England Republicans, who characterized the action as disgraceful.

But even the Exclusion Act failed to satisfy the workingmen of California, who attributed to the Chinese all the ills to be found in the corporate system of exploitation. As the Chinese were driven from the manufacturing centers, they moved to the countryside to work on farms, but the violence continued. Workers turned to the country and burned out Chinese workers, driving them away. In 1885, twenty-eight Chinese strike breakers in Rock Springs, Wyoming, were murdered by a mob. Other mobs attacked Chinese in Tacoma and Seattle, Washington.

Three years after the passage of the Exclusion Act, Chinese were no longer employed by the shoe and cigar industries of the West, but instead of bringing jobs to the white workingmen of the area, the mistreatment of the Chinese created quite another result. The cigar industry declined. The capitalists were not willing to pay the wages demanded by white workers. The shoe industry declined. The woolen industry of San Francisco died out altogether. The capitalists moved their factories elsewhere, seeking the cheap labor they had been denied.

Beginning in 1890 the terrorism against the Chinese was general in California and other states of the West. Armed mobs in the San Joaquin Valley attacked Chinese, rounded them up, put them into boxcars, and shipped them out of the area. The mobs did not care where the trains ended up—they only wanted the Chinese to be gone.

Meanwhile, the courts were in their own way augmenting the violence. In 1884 a federal court ruled that the wives of laborers who wanted to join their husbands in this country would be excluded. Other courts supported a whole series of antimiscegenation laws, which prevented Chinese (as well as blacks) from intermarrying with whites. The disgraceful

California antimiscegenation law remained on the books until 1947.

Before the turn of the twentieth century, the Exclusion Act was broadened in many ways. In 1898 the secretary of the treasury decided the act could be used to keep out, as "laborers," such people as Chinese ministers, accountants, and physicians. Indeed, John P. Irish, a San Francisco customs officer, put it very clearly one day:

> So completely are these safeguards of human liberty withdrawn that if you, sir, landed in San Francisco on a Pacific liner and had an enemy sufficiently virulent and of sufficient influence with some inspector, you could be deported as a Chinese and would find yourself utterly powerless to protect yourself or to make proof to the contrary.

One result of this attitude was to bring about a very rapid decrease in the size of the Chinese population in the United States. Some twenty thousand Chinese, who had lived here and gone back to Kwangtung Province for one reason or another, were refused reentry when they came back to the American shore. The years of repression were well begun.

Chapter Three

Chinatown, U.S.A.

Whenever any sizable group of people who share a language and cultural pattern different from the majority enter a country, they tend to congregate. They find a section of a city or a town and make it their own. It is a natural human habit, and has led to the growth of little Italys, French quarters, and Jewish ghettos in many a city. Usually, the immigrants are poor, and the section takes on their mantle over the obvious skeleton of poverty that existed before they came. Sometimes, if the group comes early enough, they may even create the character of their part of the city.

So it was with the Chinese in San Francisco more than in any other city of the United States. New York, Chicago, New Orleans, and smaller cities have their Chinese communities, but none was ever so extensive as that of San Francisco, which has always been regarded as the center of Chinese activity in the United States.

San Francisco's Chinatown grew with the bay region. The rich Chinese of what came to be known as the Six Companies built handsome shops and offices. The poor crowded together in tenements, and as time went on and the Occidental feeling against the Chinese became an overwhelming factor of life, San Francisco's Chinatown stopped being a district and became a ghetto. Around 1870 the change was obvious. Then the boundaries ran from Kearny to Powell streets and from California to Broadway; for many years these streets were to be the markers of Chinatown. Any Chinese who ventured beyond the boundaries was very likely to get in trouble. Young toughs from the Italian section called North Beach, or from other parts of San Francisco, would gang up on the Chinese and beat them, rob them, even murder them if they were found outside the lines.

From time to time the Occidentals invaded Chinatown, but the mystique of the Oriental, plus some defensive work by hired thugs and warriors, and the belief that Chinatown was full of tong hatchet men wielding guns and axes, kept the Chinese ghetto itself fairly safe.

By 1885 the pattern was almost complete. That year a public school called the Oriental School was established in Chinatown. Here the Chinese, Japanese, and Korean scholars of the city were segregated for the next twenty-five years or so.

Chinatown, San Francisco, then proceeded to become as ingrown a community as the Warsaw Ghetto. Although the cause was the local attitude rather than national attitudes or policies, the result was still the same: a state of siege. For the next quarter century, the Chinese would have the definite feeling of being walled up within an unfriendly America.

The Chinatown area in San Francisco was comprised of seven blocks. Inside those blocks thousands of people crowded into little apartments and dormitory rooms and slept in double-decker bunks. Communal uses of kitchens and bathroom facilities were the rule. The Chinese were used to lining up in the morning to use the bathroom of a house and waiting perhaps an hour to wash.

As the industries that employed the Chinese shut down, the people of Chinatown grew poorer. Only restaurants and curio shops prospered. The Six Companies seemed basically unaffected, for theirs was the world of the rich merchant. The average Chinese peasant turned immigrant-laborer had very little option. There was little work for him, and what there was paid very badly.

The Chinese who had come to America in the beginning had almost uniformly come over to raise money for their families, and they had come alone. The passage of the Exclusion Act made it impossible for them to marry and bring in a wife from China. The women who had been brought over in the 1850's and 1860's were mostly prostitutes. So the Chinatown of the turn of the twentieth century was known as "the bachelor society," because the number of men far outweighed the number of women.

Nor did the Chinese get much attention or help from the Occidentals. Only a handful of Christian missionaries offered them social services. The result of this attitude was the development in Chinatown of a tight social organization.

The first organization was the clan, or family association. Most of the American Chinese came from the Pearl River delta around Canton, and many of them were related to one another. In China a village of more than a hundred people might claim one common ancestor thirty generations back—a thousand years perhaps. The idea was staggering to Westerners, for the American nation was only about a hundred years old. But the whole concept of great age and family relationship was a dominating factor in Chinese-American life, more so even than in the old country, because the Chinese in America had to help and protect themselves in an unfriendly atmosphere.

The Wong, Lee, and Chin families were the most powerful

in Chinatown. They and lesser families set up their own social systems. They bought houses and leased apartments, and turned them into dormitories for the poor members of the clan. The men slept and ate here and cooked their own food. They shared expenses at the end of the year on the basis of ability to pay, and the rich members of the clan madc up thc difference.

Here is the recollection of Wei Bat Liu, one resident of Chinatown:

> . . . all the cousins from the Liu family in my village had one big room so all the members could fit in it, and we slept in that room, cooked in that room, one room. Anybody who had a job had to sleep outside the room, because he could afford to rent space and get a bed for himself. Anybody who couldn't find work slept in the beds in this room. . . . The ones that slept in the room most were willing to pay a little more. But even the ones who didn't sleep there were willing to pay something for the upkeep of the room.

Each clan, then, became the "family" of the resident of Chinatown. A clan secretary kept up communication with the villages back home and wrote letters for the illiterate. He also pushed the men into sending remittances back to China, into paying their debts, and into conforming with the society of Chinatown.

Above the clan level was the district level, which depended on the precise district from which the men came when they left China for America. Sze Yup, or Four Districts in Chinese, was one of these, and there were several others. The men of Sze Yup spoke the same basic dialect. They were almost all peasants, as opposed to the men of San Yup, or Three Districts, who came from an area right next to Canton. The San Yup men, being from a city region, were far more erudite, and spoke a more refined language. They were, by and large, better off financially too. The Chungshan men, on the other hand, were fishermen and farmers, and they took over the fish markets.

Each of these associations was supported by the family groups within it. The district association found jobs for its members and supplied them with room and board while they were looking for work. It also acted as a court where disputes were settled, for the Chinese virtually never went into an Occidental court. They lived quite outside the American system of law.

Through these associations and the tongs that were part of them, the Chinese in San Francisco found medical attention, money for passage home, and counseling of all kinds. If a Chinese died in America, the tong sent his body home for burial.

At the head of this structure sat the representatives of the six district associations as a supergovernment. In the 1880's the Chinese consul in San Francisco had helped the associations organize to try to fight off the Exclusion Act, and although they were not successful, the organization remained. It was called the Chinese Consolidated Benevolent Association of America or, more usually, the Six Companies. It was the congress, the president, and the supreme court all rolled into one, and it was dominated and supported by the rich merchants. The Six Companies ruled Chinatown with an iron hand. Every Chinese who went home to Kwangtung was checked at the pier to see that he had paid off all his debts. The merchants of the Six Companies collected the exit tax, which every departing Chinese paid. They imported rice and other foodstuffs from China. They made arrangements for all who were coming and going, and they worked with, and sometimes duped, the customs and immigration authorities.

The unfair and ridiculous immigration law led to so many hardships and so much confusion that the Chinese flouted it whenever they could. When the San Francisco earthquake and fire destroyed the immigration records, thousands of Chinese were able to forge birth certificates and papers so they could come to America and bring their children. Sometimes merchants were willing to be "paper fathers"—to sign papers that allowed in young men claiming to be the sons of American Chinese.

Outside the basic structure of Chinatown was another, encouraged by the high-handedness of the Six Companies. A number of independent tongs grew up. These tongs were usually illegal organizations that engaged openly in racketeering, with the connivance of crooked politicians in San Francisco's city hall. They ran the gambling halls and houses of prostitution, and smuggled opium. However, the "tong wars" of Chinatown, famous in the early years of the twentieth century, were much overrated by the sensational press of San Francisco and other cities. Average Americans, hearing the word "tong," had a vision of a Chinese, in a pigtail and pajamas, about to cleave a skull with a hatchet. The fact was, quite aside from the erroneous impression created by the press, that the average Chinese was mainly concerned with survival in an unfriendly America. Work was hard to find; the men lived in beds put against the walls like shelves; and sometimes a dormitory was so crowded they had to use the beds in shifts. For amusement they talked or played Mah-Jongg. They did very little drinking, because they had so little money. They did little gambling for the same reason. They seldom went out at night, because there was no place to go.

A good number of people were smuggled into the United States in the last years of the nineteenth century and the first years of the twentieth. The basic reason was the even harsher Scott Act of 1888, which forbade the return to the United States of any foreign laborers who had lived here and departed. Some twenty thousand Chinese were affected by this law, when their reentry permits, granted to them when they left, were declared void. Those who wanted to come back had to do it illegally.

By 1900 the census statistics of San Francisco's Chinatown and of many other Chinese communities in the United States were quite meaningless because there were so many illegal immigrants in the communities. Having sequestered the Chinese, preyed upon them, and turned them into outlaws, the American authorities had no real way of coming to grips with the illegalities of Chinatown, U.S.A. The Chinese society existed quite apart from the Americans, and the Chinese obeyed their own rules and only such federal and California laws as suited their purposes.

As a rule, events in China had much more effect on the lives of the Chinese-Americans than events in the United States. The foundations of Chinatown, U.S.A., were laid during the reign of the Manchu dynasty, when emigration was first outlawed and then frowned upon. By the time the century changed, China was in ferment, and in 1910 Dr. Sun Yat-sen, the revolutionary leader of the Kuomintang, came to America seeking support for his effort to overthrow the Manchus. He found it. His visit to Chinatown in San Francisco brought a new hope to the people there. China had been so abused by the foreigners at home and the Chinese were so abused here in America that Sun's visit was like a tonic to them. It gave hope that the Chinese could again be proud of the present and not just the past.

Dr. Sun made many speeches, and hundreds of Chinese joined his revolutionary movement. But aside from the hope he brought, the lot of the Chinese in America, and particularly in the West, remained an unhappy one.

In a way, the life of Chinatown, San Francisco, is divided into two parts: before the earthquake and after the earthquake.

Chin Hsien-sheng's life illustrates that split very well. Chin's tailoring business was making him a nice fortune in 1906, when the earthquake struck the city. His prosperity had brought him a house of his own in Chinatown. He had married and begun to raise a family.

All the Chins were in bed on the April morning in 1906 when the house began to shake. It shook out the gas light in the living room, and the house trembled so hard that pictures fell off the walls. Chin and his wife and children went to the door and looked down California Street. The wooden buildings were shivering. A huge crack in the pavement opened up before their eyes. And then the fires began. They could see the fires starting down on Montgomery Street. Soon the Merchant's Exchange Building, the largest in the financial district, was totally enveloped in flame.

Chin's tailor shop was, aptly enough, on Taylor Street, and he headed there with his family because their house had become untenable. They walked, and Chin's wife had a dreadful time. She had bound feet; when she was a baby, her mother had tied them up tightly in the Chinese fashion, and so they were less than two inches long. Walking was torture. They could go only as far as the park at Washington and Steiner streets, and there they had to stop and rest.

But they couldn't leave the park. The streets were cut off, and the city was ablaze. All night they and other Chinese stayed in the park. The next day soldiers came and took them to shelter in the Presidio, the military base on the edge of the city.

For a time after the earthquake, the Chins lived in the shrimp camps of Richmond. Then they moved up to the Sacramento River, and Chin decided to settle there. He opened a candy store in Walnut Grove and soon had another in Locke. Their son, Leland Chin, was sent to San Francisco to school because the local Caucasians would not let him go to one of their schools.

In some areas the Chinese were welcomed, particularly in

farming areas at harvest time, when the farmers and ranchers needed them. But socially they were not accepted anywhere. Too often the cry was "Chink, Chink, Chink" as they walked down the street, and they might be pelted with stones or rotten fruit.

Young Leland Chin was merely one of many thus treated. He was of an impressionable age then, and he joined the T'ung Meng Hui, which was Dr. Sun's organization. His father became interested in the movement too and subscribed a considerable sum of money to it, partly because Dr. Sun came from the Chungshan district south of Canton, and so did the Chins.

The Chinese were not totally without weapons in their unequal struggle. In 1904, when the Exclusion Act was reaffirmed and made even more onerous in some ways, the Chinese merchants on the mainland of China began to boycott American goods in protest. But the protest did not change the position of the Chinese in America, for the trouble was not in Washington, but in California and other areas, where Anglo-Saxons and other Nordic Americans were trying to convince themselves, and all others, that there was some inherent superiority in their racial makeup. This attitude was particularly strong at the lower levels of society. The Irish and other workingmen in California were the leaders of the persecution of the Chinese. The reason was almost totally economic. The rich never worried about such things as the color of a man's skin if his bankbook was green.

California was the center of the disgrace, but it was not the only place where the Chinese were hurt. Boston was the scene of one of the most disgraceful incidents in the history of Chinese-Americans. One Sunday evening police and immigration officers staged a raid on the Chinese quarter of Boston, invading every club, restaurant, public place, and even private homes, demanding to see the certificate of residence of every Chinese. No warrants were produced; no legal cause for action was ever shown. Any person who could not produce the piece of paper immediately was hustled off to jail, and some were taken off without even being asked to produce their certificates.

One old man, when asked for his certificate, said it was in a trunk upstairs and he would get it. He was given no chance, but was pushed into a truck with some eighty other persons. The truck overturned in the street, and the old man was injured. Still he was carried off and detained, even though he had a permit to be in the United States and had committed no wrong.

Some 250 Chinese were arrested in this raid and carted off to be detained in two small rooms for nearly twenty-four hours. The raid ended with 121 persons being summarily dismissed—they could find their certificates. In the end only half a dozen were deported as illegal immigrants. For so little had the whole judicial process of America been abused by the authorities.

In 1915 the Chin children moved back to Locke, California. Two years later Leland Chin was the first Chinese in the state to be drafted into the United States military service. He was sent to Camp Lewis in Washington and then to Camp Muir. Finally, he was put aboard a transport and shipped to France. He had hoped to see the world as a soldier. Instead he spent the war serving as a houseboy in an officers' training school.

The saddest part of the war to Leland Chin was his contact with the big North Chinese coolies who had been brought over to France to work on the railroads. They wore blue uniforms; they worked all day; and then at night they were herded into a stockade and locked in.

"It just kinda hurt," he said. "They're human beings, they like to have a little fun, but when they finished working, bang you go into the stockade and you're locked up until the next morning, sort of like a bunch of cattle or a bunch of horses."

Leland Chin came back from France and found that making the world safe for democracy had not made it any better for the Chinese in California. The racism continued. Leland Chin immersed himself in the community. He became a bank clerk, and he worked as a volunteer for Dr. Sun Yat-sen and eventually became a staff member of the *Young China Daily*, the Kuomintang newspaper. He was also very active in the Cathay Post of the American Legion.

So the years went by, with organized labor being notable as the most serious enemy of the Chinese. There was hardly a state labor convention in the West without the passage of an anti-Chinese resolution of some kind. California had become very racist, and the racism translated itself politically. As far as the Chinese were concerned, even after the first quarter of the twentieth century, the prejudice was unabated, and their position was scarcely improved. Only in the late 1930's, when a "greater menace" seemed to present itself, did there come a slackening of anti-Chinese feeling in California and the remainder of the West.

Chapter Four

The Japanese in America

While the Chinese were hated during the last few years of the nineteenth century, Americans were a little slower to react against the coming of the Japanese. The reason was simple enough, and can be traced. Until 1890 the Japanese had been arriving in California at the rate of about a thousand a year. This small number did not seem to pose a threat to anyone, and since the Japanese, like the Chinese, followed family and clansmen and took care of themselves, they were seldom seen.

One such family was that of Shinkichi Okomoto, who came to California from Japan before the turn of the century. His father was the third son of a farm family. He could expect no part of the family's landholdings in Japan and had to make his own way. So Shinkichi's father brought his wife and children to San Francisco. He sought work and found a job on a farm in the San Joaquin Valley.

At the age of fourteen, Shinkichi was supporting himself

as a houseboy in San Francisco. He also went to school and completed studies from the first to the eighth grade in three years, although when he arrived in San Francisco he could not speak a word of English. He got a job then as a messenger boy for an art goods store in the city. He did such things as memorize the whole city map, so he would know all the streets. Years afterward he could tell his children precisely where any numbered house was on any street.

Shinkichi wanted to become a clerk in a store, and he worked up to the job. He saved his money, and finally he opened an art goods store of his own in San Jose and began to prosper.

Other Japanese who came to America before 1900 did well too. Not all of them were poor or farmers. Mrs. Shinzo Makabe was one such. She had graduated from a Tokyo women's college and spoke fluent English, although with a British accent. She came to America to teach in a school run by missionaries in Placer County, California. One of her relatives was employed there. She also met her husband there, after he had stepped off a wagon and settled in the town of Loomis because the plum trees in bloom reminded him of home.

Their children were quickly assimilated into American society, or tried to be. They spoke English at home and learned to recite Shakespeare before they went to school. Their father was a court interpreter for the county.

Many of these Japanese had high aspirations, but often their hopes turned to dust, as with the young Japanese scion of the Yasui family of Okayama-ken in Japan. His two elder brothers had come to the West to work as section hands on the railroad. When this youngster arrived, he was offered a job as water boy. But in Japan he had hoped to become a lawyer, so he went to Portland to study law.

Then Yasui learned that he could not enter the legal profession in Oregon because he was an alien. He started east, where he had heard there was less discrimination against the Japanese. On the way his train passed through Hood River County, in the heart of the Oregon apple country. The countryside made young Yasui so homesick for Japan that he got off the train and decided to settle there. He married and raised a family of seven children.

Many of these young Japanese men came with the thought of making their fortunes and then going back to Japan. A young man named Iwakagi left his home in Wakayama late in the nineteenth century to go to California. Soon he found a job in an orchard and stayed there, living near Monterey. After fourteen years this young man decided he must have a wife, so he sent back to Wakayama and told his relatives to find him a girl. They did, and he began writing to her. After two years the couple were married in a typical Japanese ceremony, but without the presence of the groom. The bride then set sail for America and arrived on the dock wearing a Western-style dress. Her mother had told her that if they could save ten thousand yen, or about five thousand dollars, they should return to Japan. But by the time they had saved five thousand dollars, they had grown to like California, and their old homeland home seemed a long way off.

In 1900, after the annexation of Hawaii to the United States, some twelve thousand Japanese who had been living in the islands, suddenly appeared on the American shore to demand admission. The uproar began immediately.

In March Mayor James D. Phelan of San Francisco quarantined the Japanese and Chinese sections of the city. His excuse was some wild rumors that had started in the press about an epidemic of bubonic plague. The Japanese protested, but the course of anti-Oriental feeling was already marked out. In May the San Francisco Labor Council called a mass meeting against the Japanese. Labor and other racist groups began agitating for a Japanese exclusion act, which would be similar to the Chinese exclusion laws.

The Japanese government stopped issuing passports for contract laborers who wanted to go to the United States, even though various businessmen and industrialists still wanted to import them.

But this action did not satisfy organized labor. In 1901 the Chinese Exclusion League asked that the Japanese also be excluded from the United States. Three years later, at its national convention, the American Federation of Labor asked for the same thing. In 1905 the outcry against the Japanese was redoubled, and the hunt was led by the California press. The first important newspaper to begin harrying the Japanese was the San Francisco *Chronicle*. "Japanese a Menace to American Women" read one headline. "Brown Asiatics Steal Brains of Whites" said another.

Then began an unholy alliance between the racists of the Democratic Deep South and the racists of California. It was as effective in Washington, D.C., as it was in the West. As if further proof of the real roots of racism were needed, by 1905 the pressure was off the Chinese because they had been driven into the ghettos and their expansion had stopped. The pressure was now on the Japanese. In March, 1905, the two houses of the California legislature voted *unanimously* to urge Congress to exclude all Japanese. What author Carey McWilliams later described as "California's war with Japan" began then. A Japanese and Korean Exclusion League was formed in San Francisco.

President Theodore Roosevelt tried to stop this growth of racism, but he met with no success west of the Rockies. A strange combination of labor, antilabor, and the crooked politicians of San Francisco combined to make the Oriental problem the whipping boy of California politics, and out of this combination arose a nativist, jingoist, racist organization called the Sons of the Golden West, which became the driving force in California politics for nearly two decades. (This was also the period in which the Ku Klux Klan was revived in the South and Midwest as an antiforeign and anti-Catholic organization.)

In 1906 the San Francisco school board ordered all Oriental students in the city to attend the segregated school in Chinatown. The "menace" of the Japanese in the city was tremendous: There were ninety-three Japanese students out of a total school population of twenty-five thousand students. Japanese parents refused to send their children to a segregated school, and the Japanese consul made protests in Washington.

When fire and earthquake destroyed much of San Francisco that year, a good deal of the Japanese community around Eddy Street was wiped out. Ten thousand Japanese residents lost their houses and apartments. The Japanese organized immediately for relief, under K. Uyeno, the Japanese consul. Ten Japanese doctors donated their services and set up emergency stations at Fort Mason, in Lafayette Square in the center of the city, and at the Japanese Tea Garden. The businessmen began sending the homeless away from the city, and in ten days seven thousand Japanese refugees moved into the interior of California. The Japanese government and the Red Cross combined forces to help these people, and the Japanese government sent half a million dollars for general earthquake relief to San Francisco. Yet the anti-Japanese forces were on the move, and the Japanese Exclusion League indicated its hopes that the Japanese who had gone away would never come back.

Thus began a change in the friendly feelings that had guided Japanese-American relations until this time. In Tokyo the agitation in California aroused such resentment that

Mainichi Shimbun, which was as nationalistic in its way as the San Francisco *Chronicle,* suggested that the Japanese send warships to San Francisco to protect the Japanese there.

President Theodore Roosevelt disapproved of all the agitation and sent the secretary of commerce and labor to investigate the goings-on in San Francisco. But California locked arms with Alabama and the other states of the Deep South. The Southern segregationists knew that if Roosevelt could stop segregation in California, he could also stop it in their region, and they fought him tooth and nail. They began talking in Washington about war with Japan.

California won the battle. President Roosevelt agreed to negotiate with Japan for suspension of immigration if San Francisco would stop subverting the American constitution. It is true—that is what happened—and in 1907 Japan and the United States entered a "Gentlemen's Agreement" under which the Japanese government limited the passports of those who wished to go to the Western Hemisphere and tried to control the process by which Japanese went to Mexico or other countries and then moved to the United States.

How close the United States and Japan came to war then will never be known. President Roosevelt believed war was imminent. Later, Japanese historians reported that had their country not been recovering from the cost of the Russo-Japanese War at that time, they would have declared war on the United States. Certainly, the anti-Japanese rioting and newspaper publicity of these years added to the strength of the jingos who were seizing control of Japanese policy.

Anti-Oriental feeling received support in some very strange places in those years before World War I. Woodrow Wilson is generally regarded as an internationalist and liberal. Yet when he went to California during the presidential campaign of 1912 he said that America would never assimilate the Oriental population. "We cannot make a homogeneous population of a people who do not blend with the Caucasian race." That homogeneity—or the creation of one mold from which all Americans would be stamped—was the aim of most of America in those days. So what Wilson was saying in effect was that Orientals could not be assimilated; therefore, they must go. The statement was so credited and was so used by California racists.

California's sniping at the Orientals continued. Although the Wilson Administration tried to stop it, in 1913 the legislature passed an Alien Land Act, which prohibited land ownership by "aliens ineligible for citizenship." This meant the Orientals and particularly the Japanese. Most of the racism of California stemmed from the farmers and laborers, while the big landowners and industrialists were antiracist because they had the most to gain through the employment of cheap labor.

World War I brought a temporary end to racial strife in California and anti-Orientalism in America, because Japan and China were on the side of the Western Allies. Chinese laborers were brought to France to work as coolies, unloading supplies for the western front. American Chinese and Japanese enlisted or were conscripted into the armed forces. As usual, what was seen as the greater danger wiped out the "menace" of the Orientals.

But anti-Orientalism and particularly anti-Japanese agitation did not stop. The leader now became William Randolph Hearst, who was accumulating a string of newspapers across the United States. Hearst was pro-German and anti-Japanese, and Hearst had many other ways of using his influence besides the press. He owned control of some motion-picture companies, and he used them to make racist films. His agitation was joined by others, including V. S. McClatchy, owner of three important newspapers in the San Joaquin Valley. Oddly enough, by the middle of the 1920's, as anti-Japanese feeling steadily rose, racism against the Chinese began to reverse itself.

In 1923 the Alien Land Act was declared constitutional, and it became a model for nearly every state in the West during the 1920's. Japanese owned some 360,000 acres of land in California, and of course this amount began to decline. The whites had complained that the Japanese dominated the production of vegetables and some fruits, but once the Japanese left the land, the whites found they could not match the farming techniques of the Japanese. For hundreds of years Japanese farmers had been producing a large number of crops from limited land. They did it by intensive farming and very hard work—an effort the Occidentals were not willing to make for so little in return.

For instance, the Katai family, who lived in Montebello, a suburb of Los Angeles, had come to California from the island of Shikoku, where they had been farmers. They worked hard in the United States. The father and mother walked for miles from the house to the fields they used every day. The mother carried the latest baby on her back, Japanese style, then put the child down and cautioned an older child to watch it while she worked.

Some of the older children were left at home to tend the house and do the washing and cleaning. Yuri Katai, the second-oldest daughter, did much of the washing, but sometimes she also worked in the fields, picking strawberries, planting celery, harvesting broccoli. The whole Katai family worked, and they were happy even though they were poor. They could do more with their small piece of land than many Caucasians could do with ten times as much.

The severe Immigration Act of 1924 discriminated terribly against all Orientals. Chinese and Japanese wives of Americans were not to be allowed in the United States, and all aliens ineligible for citizenship were to be thrown out of the country.

In Japan the reaction to the new law was sharp and severe. Two Japanese committed suicide in protest, and their funeral in Tokyo inspired a huge popular demonstration against the United States. It was the most damaging blow yet to Japanese-American relations, and it so hurt industry and the big farmers in California that they began agitating through the Chamber of Commerce for less harsh laws.

The American Depression of the 1930's heightened anti-Japanese feeling, because Japanese manufacturers had begun to take away American markets abroad. However, feeling against the Japanese also grew stronger for quite another reason. In 1931 the Japanese had started to take over Manchuria. Already they had seized Formosa and Korea and had wrung many concessions from the weak Chinese government. Now the Japanese army clique began to move to make China a Japanese colony.

By this time Japanese and Chinese had been in America for nearly half a century, and some vital changes had come in their family ways and in their attitudes. The original Japanese, like the original Chinese, had come to the United States and Hawaii to make a nest egg, with every intention of returning to the homeland. But some settled down and in one way or another managed to bring wives to this new country. The *Issei,* who were born in Japan, thought often of the homeland, but their children were *Nisei*—they were born in America. Most of the Nisei spoke some Japanese at home, but at school and in what they saw and read their outlook was American. They went to American movies. They read American magazines. They considered themselves to be Americans. Yet America had no real place for them.

The Nisei went to college, but when they graduated, they discovered, like the Chinese, that they could not get jobs in the United States. One Nisei boy who graduated with honors from a Midwestern university went out to find a job in his specialty—electrical engineering. He finally got a job in Los Angeles, not as an engineer, but as journeyman electrician—a trade, not a profession.

Shiju Hirabayashi, a Japanese-American girl who graduated with a degree in education in 1939 from San Jose State College, tried to find work as a teacher and could not. So she trained as a secretary so she could take a more menial job. The same story was repeated a thousand times. Orientals were simply not wanted in positions of trust or importance in the general community.

Yet while the majority of the Japanese immigrants in America were truck gardeners, grocers, agricultural workers, fishermen, or cannery workers, their children had other ideas. In 1940 almost half of the young Nisei on the West Coast of the United States were students. They were more interested in seeking positions in the general world than in finding jobs in the narrow Japanese-American world. Whatever quarrel the general American public had with them because of their "difference," the Nisei's major quarrel was with their senior Japanese. The Nisei spoke English fluently; they had adopted American customs, usually to the disgust of their seniors; and they were drawing apart from the world of Japan.

Some Nisei were sent or went gladly to Japan to study, particularly at the university level, but in Japan they were regarded with suspicion because of their American ways and American outlook on the world. By the late 1930's the Nisei were beginning to assimilate into American society in a way that the jingoists had said could never be done. Some voices were being raised in their behalf in the United States, even in California. Sociologists began to point out that in a high-crime period the Japanese and Chinese had very little crime, and they praised Oriental standards of family life.

The Nisei were truly integrating into American life, and some writers indicate that had they been given three or four more years before World War II—another college generation—affairs might have turned out a good deal differently than they did for the Japanese in America.

However, they were not given the time. Political considerations began to take precedence over social factors. Japanese aggression against China and a well-financed campaign of propaganda in America against Japanese expansion brought new emotions. The Chinese suddenly found themselves more acceptable to Occidental Americans than ever before, while the Japanese became objects of deep suspicion. When Japan joined the Berlin-Rome Axis in 1940, the suspicion increased. Americans broke off the treaty with Japan that covered commercial and agricultural rights. California, always the leader of anti-Oriental hysteria, passed laws that were supposed to offer protection against Japanese spies, sabotage, and subversive activity.

In July, 1941, Japanese bank accounts in the United States were frozen, and the American-Japanese had to take their birth certificates and records of citizenship to their banks to get their accounts unfrozen. Japanese ships stopped calling at American ports. Americans were urged to leave Japan and Japanese-occupied territory. Then came that fateful day, December 7, 1941, and the Japanese attack on Pearl Harbor.

Chapter Five

The Indians in Africa

Just as the Indians went to Africa for the same reasons that Chinese and Japanese came to the United States, so these Asians were treated in almost precisely the same way once they arrived, settled in, and began to adopt the new country as their own.

The government of India was not very eager to see the Indians go, knowing what was happening elsewhere in the world, but in the beginning the conditions of the Asian contract workers in Africa seemed fairly good. They were guaranteed three-year indenture, no more, and then free passage home if they wished it. If not, they could remain two more years and choose their own employer. If they chose not to take the free passage home, they were entitled to a free grant of Crown land.

All went well until it became obvious that practically none of these Indians were opting to return home after they finished their service. They had been brought over by the planters as "cheap labor." They remained to become part of the country. They grew maize, or corn, and tobacco so successfully that others could not compete with them. Like the Japanese and the Chinese, they were used to intensive cultivation methods, for in their homeland men had to make use of every available foot of ground. As the Asians in Africa prospered, they aroused the envy of the less successful whites, and the old story was enacted once again.

The Orange Free State sternly forbade the entrance of any more Asians. The colony of Natal began to impose restrictive laws on the Indians.

In America the growth of the Chinese colony in particular had been stemmed by the practice of bringing in only male workers. But the Indian government had insisted that the contract laborers going to Africa be accompanied by women—forty women to every hundred men was the rule. So some of the Indians were able to find wives in Africa without going home for them, and this speeded the development of the Asian population there. Soon there were around a hundred thousand people from various parts of India in the South African colonies.

By 1890 a definite pattern of repression had set in. The whites, who also discriminated severely against the blacks, called the Indians coolies. Most hotels would not accept Indian guests. Usually, if an Indian walked into a dining room, he would not be served: if he was, the Occidental guests might get up and leave. If Indians rode on the railroads, they were supposed to ride third class and not consider themselves in any way the equals of the whites.

This attitude was not held by all African whites by any means, any more than anti-Orientalism ever represented the view of all Americans. But because Occidental politics depends on an appeal to common interests, the policy of the South African governments degenerated into a defense of the "poor white," who felt he had to have some basis for feeling superior to someone. Indians and native Africans became the butt of this abuse.

But there was a basic difference between the situation of the Asians in Africa and that of the Orientals in America. China and Japan were both weak nations when their people began to move to the West. India was a part of the British Empire, and its government and citizens had a special relationship with all other parts of the Empire.

Also the Chinese and the Japanese in America had no strong political organization or spokesman. The Indians of Africa were to develop a leader.

In the fall of 1893—the month of May being fall in South Africa—a young bespectacled Indian barrister who had trained in London arrived in Durban by ship. He had come to help a wealthy Indian merchant recover some property that had been misused. He arrived in Western clothes and with many Western habits. In London this young man had been well treated, and he had been educated in the highest tradition of the British law. Returning to India, he had been appalled at the mistreatment of Indians in their own land by the British officers, and he had accepted gladly a commission to go to South Africa to work for a time. This young man was Mohandas Karamchand Gandhi, son of a well-known Indian official, but a man who seemed to bear little promise of greatness himself.

Gandhi, however, was a stubborn young man and a great lover of India. In Durban, when a magistrate insisted that he remove his turban in the courtroom, Gandhi refused. It was not the Indian custom to remove one's turban. He left the room rather than conform. Muslims were allowed to wear their turbans for religious reasons, but the Hindus received no respect in Africa. Gandhi decided to fight. The story of his life in Africa illustrates what can happen when a minority group acquires a strong leader.

From Durban young Gandhi set out by train for Pretoria.

He had a first-class ticket on the train, and rode in a first-class compartment. When the train reached Maritzburg, an attendant ordered him to go into third class. He refused. The trainman called a policeman, and Gandhi was put off the train. He sent a telegram to the manager of the railroad and one to his rich merchant friend. The next night a train arrived bound toward Pretoria with a reserved first-class compartment on it for him.

The railroad ran only to Charlestown. There he had to take a stagecoach. The agent, who was riding in the coach, first refused to let Gandhi sit inside, so he sat on the box with the coachman. Then the agent decided he wanted to sit on the box, and he ordered Gandhi to sit on the floorboards. When Gandhi refused, the agent began beating him and stopped only when ordered to do so by other whites. Gandhi did not fight back.

Finally, Gandhi reached Johannesburg. He went to a hotel, where he was immediately refused admission. Asians were not allowed in hotels.

When Gandhi described this experience to a merchant acquaintance who knew the ways of Africa, the merchant just laughed. "Only *we* can live in a land like this," he said, "because for making money we do not mind pocketing insults, and here we are."

Gandhi bought another first-class ticket to Pretoria, set out, and a guard tried to put him out of the compartment. Only the interference of an Englishman, who said he had no objection to Gandhi's riding with him, saved the Indian from further trouble.

"If you want to travel with a coolie, what do I care?" said the trainman. But he left them alone.

In Pretoria there were further humiliations, for in 1893 white South Africans were very much concerned lest the Indians take over their new land. The more the shrewd and hardworking Indian businessmen prospered, the more the less prosperous whites complained. Gandhi had nowhere to go. A black American in Pretoria station directed him to a hotel run by an American, but even at Johnson's Family Hotel, the proprietor was afraid to let Gandhi eat in the dining room until he had canvassed his other guests to see if they objected.

They did not object at all—and that is one of the most interesting aspects of prejudice. Having been told that Gandhi was a distinguished, English-trained barrister, the guests did not mind sharing the dining room with him, but had they walked in to see a dark-skinned Indian eating there, many of them might have walked out, as Mr. Johnson had feared. Economic fear and blind fear of people who are different were again, in South Africa, the cornerstones of prejudice.

What was new in the African experience in 1893 was not what happened to Gandhi, but his reaction to it, as suggested by B. R. Nanda, Gandhi's biographer. Other Indians simply accepted the white man's intolerance. Gandhi bridled and decided to fight it.

Since 1888 Indians had been deprived of all rights by the Orange Free State. The Transvaal taxed Indians for the right to enter the state. For all practical purposes, Indians could not own land. They could not even use land except in specially selected areas. They could not vote. They could not go out of doors from nine o'clock at night until after dawn without carrying a special pass that showed who they were and what their business was.

As Gandhi was preparing to leave South Africa, he learned of a bill in the Natal legislature that would take the vote away from Indian settlers, and he decided to stay on and fight for his countrymen in the new land. He began a campaign as a publicist, writing pamphlets and making speeches. The plight of the Indian in Africa became well known in the British Empire, better known, in fact, than the situation of the Chinese or Japanese in America. But Gandhi's work did not deter the whites of South Africa from their course. His fight aroused grave interest in India and other parts of the Empire and made Gandhi an important figure in India and South Africa, but it did not stop the disfranchisement of Indians in Natal.

Still, Gandhi was not dismayed. He began to promote a petition to the Crown. Under Empire law the bills passed by colonial legislatures had to be sent to the colonial secretary, and they had to be accepted by the government in London before they became law. Because of the agitation stirred up by Gandhi, the British government vetoed the Natal legislation.

Undeterred, the legislature changed the law a little—just enough to remove the words that discriminated against the inhabitants of another part of the British Empire—and passed it again. For all practical purposes, the Indians lost the right to vote. And they could not trade without a license, which was granted for the asking to an Occidental, but not to an Indian. They could not remain in South Africa either unless they could pass the literacy test in English.

These restrictions did not apply to the indentured laborers as long as they worked as virtual slaves, but it kept them from remaining on as free men and settling down in the country. There were, around the turn of the century, about a hundred thousand Indians in South Africa, and the Boers and Englishmen were afraid they would soon take over the country. The Indians were successful traders, and they had made themselves indispensable in the growth of the nation. That did not help them, however, or decrease the hatred or the use of the word "coolie" to describe any Oriental.

Gandhi was instrumental in the organization of the Natal Indian Congress, which became the spokesman for the Indians of the land. This organization was a pressure group that exerted influence on the outside world, the governments of South Africa, and the Indian community.

For the next three years Gandhi stayed on in South Africa fighting the battle of his fellow Indians. He returned to India briefly in 1896 to bring back his wife and family, but in India he continued to pamphleteer and work for the people who had gone to Africa. The news of his work got back to Natal, and when he returned, the whites chose him as their worst enemy, a symbol of all they hated about the Indians.

Gandhi was accused of having organized an agency in India to flood Natal with Indian immigrants. This charge seemed plausible, for it happened that the ship on which Gandhi was traveling and another owned by his friend Abdallah Sheth, a merchant, bore nearly five hundred immigrants. Some two thousand whites gathered in Durban to protest the coming of these Indians and to promise them free return passage if they would go home. After threatening the shipowners and hinting at violence, they secured a quarantine of the ships that lasted three weeks.

Finally, on January 13, 1897, the ships entered Durban Harbor and were met by a crowd of four thousand angry Europeans. The other Indians disembarked, but the authorities asked Gandhi to wait for nightfall, when the chief of police would come and get him and protect him. But Gandhi decided it would be undignified to slip away like a thief, so he left the ship with an Occidental friend. He was attacked by the mob, kicked, and pelted with stones and rotten eggs. His friend was torn away and Gandhi was left alone. He had given up all hope of reaching home alive when the wife of the superintendent of police, Mrs. Alexander, came by and saw what was happening. She walked to Gandhi's side, shielded him from the eggs and fruit with her parasol, and kept the infuriated Europeans at bay.

Gandhi went to stay with a friend, but in a few hours more members of the mob came and surrounded the house. They threatened to burn it if Gandhi did not come out and surrender to them. Superintendent Alexander went out and argued with the mob while Gandhi was dressed in the uniform of an Indian policeman and spirited out of the house.

In a day or two law was again returned to Natal. In London the secretary of state for the colonies demanded the prosecution of Gandhi's assailants, but Gandhi said the fault was not with a few hotheads but with the responsible men who had stirred them up. Neither then nor ever would Gandhi hold individuals responsible for such acts when they were the tools of others.

Gandhi continued to organize the Indian community. Soon he was faced with a major political decision. The outbreak of the Boer War in 1899 forced a declaration of attitude by the Indians. Were they for the British, who had mistreated them, or would they remain neutral and hope the Boers won? Many Indians argued for neutrality. Gandhi argued for service. The British did not want the help of the untrained Indians, but as the war progressed, Gandhi and others were allowed to form an ambulance corps, which worked along the front lines of the fighting.

At the end of the war, Gandhi returned to India once more, but in a year the Indian community called him back to South Africa, for instead of becoming better because of the Indians' war service, the conditions of the Asians were growing worse. Before, the British of Natal had mistreated the Indians. Now the British, having taken over the old Boer Transvaal area, began enforcing very severe restrictions on Indians there.

Gandhi tried to see the British authorities who were traveling in India that winter of 1902, but they would not talk to him. A new period of repression of the Indians began.

In 1905 some hotheads raised the threat of an Indian invasion of South Africa. The Indian government was secretly smuggling people into the country, they said, and planned to overrun the South African colonies in the next few years.

The Transvaal was the center of this hysteria, even though the Indian colony in the Transvaal was smaller in 1905 than it had been in 1899, when the Transvaal was a Boer state.

By this time the Indians had been in Africa for fifty years, and many of them were third generation. They considered the African colonies their home.

Gandhi and others offered to put an end to the importation of Indian contract workers. All the Indians of South Africa wanted was the right to live in their new country in peace and with the dignity and self-respect offered to others. But that was just what the white South Africans did not want. They did not mind Indian contract workers, who were not much better than slaves, as long as they would go home when their contract ended and not settle down to become citizens of South Africa.

A new campaign of repression began, aimed at forcing the Indians to leave South Africa. At a meeting in Johannesburg on September 11, 1906, Gandhi opened a campaign of civil disobedience against the hated Asiatic registration law, which held that every Indian in the colonies affected must be registered and prepared to show his permit at all times. Thus came into being Gandhi's famous principle of Satyagraha, which in Hindustani means firmness in good conduct. Sometimes it was called passive resistance. The idea was to disobey the law, but to offer no violence to those who enforced it.

In the summer of 1907 the permit offices were opened, but the Indians boycotted them. Transvaal authorities managed to persuade only five hundred Indians to register. The rest would not. Gandhi was sent to jail for two months. The Johannesburg jail began to fill with Indians.

General Jan Christiaan Smuts, leader of the government, called Gandhi in and made a compromise with him, which Gandhi accepted. The Indians would register and the government would remove the law. But Smuts reneged on the agreement, and Gandhi was attacked and nearly killed by Indians who claimed he had betrayed them.

The repressive measures continued, and the Satyagraha struggle went on for seven years. Finally, the Transvaal government agreed to take off the restrictive measures, but the harrying of the Asians went on. The government was constantly passing new laws to make life difficult for them. For example, Asiatic limitation was no longer accomplished by registration, but by a severe education test. The courts even held at one time that all Hindu, Muslim, and Parsi marriages were invalid.

Gandhi led strikes and marches against the governments of Natal and the Transvaal. He was imprisoned, but in the end his campaign won certain rights for the Indians. The three-pound tax was abolished. Marriages were made legal even though they were not Christian. The hated registration laws were dropped.

The Indians still lived in a ghetto; they still had trouble moving from one colony to another; they still had special trade restrictions, taxes, and licenses; they still could not own land. But Gandhi hoped these wrongs would soon be righted, and he left South Africa in 1914, full of hope for the future of his kinsmen in their new country.

Chapter Six

The Japanese in World War II

White American racial intolerance against minorities continued very largely unabated until the opening days of World War II, and though the Chinese gained a certain grudging respect with the fight of Chiang Kai-shek and his people against the Japanese invaders, the Japanese in America took all the venom that was left over from the miserable treatment of American blacks.

World War II brought a crisis for the Japanese in America. The attack on Pearl Harbor shocked Japanese-Americans as much as it did anyone else in the country. A few who had traveled to Japan in recent years had suspected that war was coming, but not many. The Nisei, in particular, were no better informed about Japanese-American relations than their Occidental teen-age and college friends.

On Pearl Harbor day San Francisco declared a state of emergency, and Mayor Angelo Rossi blocked off all traffic into the Japanese section of the city. In Los Angeles extra police went to Little Tokyo to protect the Japanese against possible trouble. There were 47,000 Japanese immigrants in the United States and 112,000 persons of Japanese descent. There was no outstanding Japanese leader.

Immediately, a number of Japanese, suspected of working for the new enemy, were arrested by the American authorities. The FBI pounced down on businessmen and fishermen. Seiichi Nakahara, a San Pedro ship chandler, was arrested because he had supplied Japanese ships with goods, because he had recently visited Japan, because he was interested in short-wave radio, and because he had received a telegram a few days earlier from Japanese Ambassador Kichisaburo Nomura, who was a kinsman of his family. Such flimsy circumstantial evidence was more than enough to detain a Japanese-American in 1941.

Some Japanese brought trouble on themselves, without a doubt. In the farming community of Guadeloupe, a number of Issei got together when they heard of the attack on Pearl Harbor and cheered. That kind of action did not help matters a bit, and most of them were soon arrested. But so were others whose only loyalty was to the United States.

Difficult as the Japanese position was at the outbreak of the war, it soon became much worse. The West Coast was declared a theater of war, and on January 29, 1942, all enemy aliens were forbidden to enter such important places as harbors, airports, and the areas around power stations.

Martial law was proclaimed in Hawaii, which meant that the whole territory came under military jurisdiction. Soon the military authorities on the West Coast of the United States were demanding the ouster of the Japanese, and by midsummer of that year all Japanese—which meant persons of Japanese ancestry, not just Japanese citizens—were moved out of Washington, Oregon, California, and parts of Arizona. The reason given for their removal was fear of invasion. There was another reason as well, but it was based on a total misconception. General J. L. DeWitt was concerned about espionage activity on the West Coast. There *was* such espionage, which included the signaling to submarines at sea, *but it was not conducted by Japanese*. Later it was shown that the spies were mostly American-born agents of Japan and Nazi Germany, none of them Oriental.

The real reason for the evacuation of the Japanese from the West Coast was almost purely racial. Military and naval officers had for years been practicing for a war against Japan. The enemy in the various American war plans for the Pacific was called Orange, and Orange was obviously imperial Japan. Such military leaders as General DeWitt and Admiral William Halsey shared one deep-seated belief about the Japanese. General DeWitt put it succinctly in testimony before the House of Representatives Naval Affairs Subcommittee:

> A Jap's a Jap. They are a dangerous element, whether loyal or not. There is no way to determine their loyalty. . . . It makes no difference whether he is an American; theoretically he is still a Japanese. . . . You can't change him by giving him a piece of paper.

The evacuation of the Japanese from their homes was a frighteningly easy matter. Since the Japanese had to register, the federal government had a list of more than seven thousand Japanese-owned farms, and they totaled some 258,000 acres. The Japanese were told they had to sell and get out. At the same time they were asked to keep on supplying the United States military with vegetables as long as they stayed on. Thus the Navy told Takeo Yuchi, a Salinas farmer, to keep supplying the Navy with onions, and he did so until the day he was forced off his land.

The one protection for the Japanese farmers was the Farm Security Administration, whose agents tried to keep the land hungry from gouging the Japanese, but that was not always possible. Occidental farmers paid the Japanese ridiculously low prices for their farm equipment, and the Japanese had to take what they were offered, because there was no other market. One Salinas farmer had spent $125 an acre to put in his garlic crop; he had to sell the crop for $100 an acre. Some farmers had to forfeit the money they had put up to lease land. Some lost their land because they could not meet the mortgage payments.

In the cities it was as bad or worse. Whole areas suddenly went up for sale. In Phoenix, Henry Takemori, who had spent years building a grocery business, sold it for $800. That was about what he had paid for his new meat counter. In San Francisco junk dealers roamed the streets of the Japanese section, buying up property at bargain rates. They "helped" the Japanese by paying $5 for a washing machine, or $20 for a new refrigerator.

The hysteria was fanned by the newspapers, and sometimes the results would have been ludicrous had they not been so sad. For such Japanese-Americans as Kiyoshi Patrick Okura they were tragic.

Okura was a Nisei graduate of the University of California at Los Angeles who had a job as a civil service technician with the Los Angeles city government. His task was to test job applicants, and the Civil Service Commission was satisfied with his work. But when the hysteria began, columnist Drew Pearson decided he would "expose" this wicked "Jap." He charged that in Los Angeles a Japanese posing as an Irishman named K. Patrick O'Kura had wormed his way into the city government and had established a ring of fifty saboteurs, who were ready to blow up the water system at the right time.

There was one fact here (as there sometimes was in Pearson's stories). The fact was that Okura existed and that in the course of time some fifty Japanese-Americans had been employed by the city government, some of them in the water department. All the rest was fiction.

After Pearson made the charge on his weekly radio broadcast, Mayor Fletcher Bowron's aides suggested it would be nice if the Irish O'Kura were to disappear, which could be accomplished by the Japanese Okura's resignation. Okura refused to resign until someone told him what he had done that was wrong.

Mayor Bowron was not one to swim against the tide. He personally asked Okura to resign, and again Okura refused. This young Nisei was very popular among his co-workers—indeed, the "Irish" angle to Drew Pearson's story came from the fact that many of Okura's friends called him the Japanese Irishman because of his name. Those friends now stood up and announced that the whole department would resign, en masse, if Okura was fired. So he was not fired. The problem was solved when the word came that all people of Japanese descent were to be sent to concentration camps.

The Japanese were assembled in various places. Santa Anita race track was one concentration camp, and Tanforan near San Francisco was another. The Japanese could take their bedding and toilet articles and whatever else they wanted, as long as it did not come to more than the contents of two suitcases and one seabag per person. When they entered the concentration camps, their names were replaced by numbers. They were kept behind barbed wire, and soldiers with bayonets guarded the towers and the gates.

Occidental Americans, for the most part, knew nothing about the camps. They learned through the press that the Japanese had been "relocated" and were living in "relocation centers." What they did not know was the similarity between these centers and Adolf Hitler's concentration camps in Germany. True, the Japanese were not murdered in the camps, but neither were the internees of the Germans in the beginning. The frightening thing about the treatment of the Japanese was that it occurred without stirring any fuss in the general community. This fact presents a matter for other generations of Americans to ponder. Just how far can a government go in repressing an unpopular segment of the population before the public takes some responsibility? The Americans of the 1940's usually claimed ignorance of the fate of the Japanese in the United States during the war, just as the Germans of the 1940's claimed after the war that they had known nothing of the brutality of Adolf Hitler and the Nazis.

Living conditions in the relocation centers were hardly ideal. A family of eight was given a room twenty feet long and twenty feet wide, about twice as much room as a farmer gives his sheep. At Tanforan race track families lived in the horse stables. Twenty-five stalls were condemned, but the government continued to use them to house these prisoners. Some women hated the night because that was when the rats came out.

There *were* protests. In the summer of 1942 *The New Republic* published an angry article about the "concentration camps," but few Americans paid any attention. The Army complained about the article, so the editors of the magazine sent a man to investigate, and he temporized, saying the conditions were only temporary.

But conditions were very bad. Sometimes there was not enough food. Sometimes it was inedible. The government first allowed about thirty-five cents per evacuee for each day's food. This was not enough, and it was later increased to fifty cents; but the quality was usually poor and the quantity often insufficient.

The conditions persisted. The American press has proudly claimed for itself the guardianship of freedoms, but in the case of the American Japanese, the press was almost totally blind. The Los Angeles *News,* the San Francisco *Chronicle,* and the San Francisco *Daily News* did expose the evils of the camps, but most papers, particularly the Hearst newspapers and the powerful Los Angeles *Times,* were on the side of repression. They did not report the news of the camps, although they "made" other news by inflating rumors and exaggerating facts.

At first, the Army took Nisei as draftees and enlistees. But by June, 1942, Japanese-Americans were being categorically turned away as 4-F, which meant undesirable, or 4-C, which meant aliens unacceptable for service. Those Nisei who were in the Army were transferred to posts far inland, and several hundred were given honorable discharges. The others were assigned to noncombat duty.

In the fall of 1942, the government decided the Japanese would all be moved to other concentration camps inland, so they could not possibly endanger anything or anybody. Most of the inland places chosen were in the desert. In the Mohave Desert was the community of Poston, which had three big camps, nicknamed by the inmates "Roaston," "Toaston," and "Duston" because of the heat and dusty sand, which caused seven of the newcomers to die very soon of heat exhaustion. The survivors sprayed water in their rooms and wet the cots and carried towels around their heads when they went out in the blazing sun. Even the guards began to come down with heat prostration; one of them died of it.

The camps were concentration camps, and they offered no comfort. Because of the sand and dust, the women could not keep the floors of their barracks-type buildings clean. When it rained, the camp became a great mud puddle.

In all, the Japanese were confined to ten camps. Gila River in Arizona was one of the best of them. Yuri Katai and her family ended up there. She and her brothers and sisters used to go to outdoor movies. They sat on a hill on an army blanket and watched the pictures on the big screen through the organ-pipe cactuses.

Within a matter of months after Pearl Harbor high authorities began to understand that they actually needed the Nisei and Kibei (Japanese-Americans who had studied in Japan). Practically no other Americans could speak Japanese. In fact, even many of the Nisei could not speak the language fluently.

The Army began to recruit Nisei for language work. The Navy used them only to instruct others in the language, for the Navy's distrust of anything Japanese was deep-seated.

The position of the United States was made very difficult when the Nazis began trumpeting that the war in the Pacific was a racial war. Enemy propaganda was designed to turn the neutral and the colonial peoples of Asia against the United States. Elmer Davis, director of the United State Office of War Information, saw the danger. He urged President Franklin Roosevelt to accept Nisei for general service in the Army. The Marine Corps had some Nisei, but was not comfortable with them. Very few had managed to gain admission to the Air Force and still fewer to the Coast Guard.

Early in 1943, however, Secretary of War Henry Stimson announced that he was planning the organization of a new military unit, a special combat team of Nisei. Already there existed one Nisei unit, the 100th Infantry Battalion. This unit had been a Hawaiian National Guard Unit, activated into the Army. Now Stimson would form the 442nd Battalion, consisting of forty-five hundred men.

Immediately the volunteers came forth. From Hawaii, 7500 Nisei volunteered for the special unit, although the Hawaiian quota was supposed to be only 1500. From behind the barbed wire of the concentration camps, only 1100 volunteered, although the Army had wanted to get 3000 men there. The low number was a commentary on the feelings of the Japanese-Americans who had been so mistreated by their fellows. Some Japanese within the camps developed very strong feelings against the American government because of their treatment. Crime increased, and politeness decreased. These people were not likely to remain valuable citizens under such conditions.

But the Nisei who were in the Army made a deep and lasting mark for themselves as loyal American soldiers. The 100th Battalion sailed for North Africa in August, 1943, and joined the Allied forces in the invasion of Salerno. That unit also fought in four engagements along the Volturno River and in the assault on Monte Cassino, the stoutly defended monastery that held out against siege for such a long time. In 1944 Lt. Gen. Mark Clark gave the 100th Battalion a Distinguished Unit Citation.

The 442nd Combat Team became the most decorated unit in the United States Army and was conspicuous for the bravery and ability of its men. They won more than a thousand medals and citations.

From their training days, the men of the 442nd had a high morale. Their unit's motto was "Go for broke." In the youthful slang of the 1940's, the motto meant they were willing to die to prove their loyalty to their country. In training, the Nisei had some odd surprises. They trained at Camp Shelby, Mississippi, where they were befriended by many people. When they went into town, they would see signs that said "colored" and others that said "white." Since they were not white, they would use the colored entrances; then the whites would tell them they were not colored, and it was all right to use the white entrance. It was very confusing, but what it came down to was the same old story of segregation. There were so few Japanese in the American South that no one regarded them as a threat; therefore, there was no racial animosity. They were accepted as ordinary human beings—a little different perhaps, but just people like the whites who had put up the segregating signs.

These Nisei went on to Europe to fight bravely and well and to make history at Bruyeres, France, where they gained a reputation for never giving up. The casualty rate of the unit was 308 percent, but in a way it was worth it. The Japanese-Americans gained a reputation for being sturdy, loyal fighters. When the 442nd came home in 1946, it marched down Constitution Avenue in Washington, and President Truman himself gave the unit its Distinguished Unit Citation. As one Nisei of the 442nd said with some satisfaction at the end of the war, they were probably the only group of American soldiers who got precisely what they fought for. They went to war to win the respect and admiration of their fellow Americans, and they did so, through their own brave efforts.

The men of the 442nd and the 100th battalions were not the only Nisei who served honorably and well. Some six thousand Japanese-Americans went to war in the Pacific theater, where they were in much more danger, if much more needed. Most of them served in military intelligence or related fields, and so their work was secret for the most part until the end of the war. There was no Nisei unit in the Pacific, and the reason was logical. Top-ranking officers feared that if they sent a Nisei unit into battle, the Japanese enemy might get the idea of putting soldiers in American uniforms and creating tremendous confusion. But the Nisei were there. Fourteen of them fought with Brig. Gen. Frank Merrill in his campaign behind the Japanese lines in Burma in 1943. Others served with intelligence units and propaganda units.

Hoichi Kubo was one of those who fought in the Pacific. One day in the battle for Saipan, he went down a hundred-foot cliff on a rope alone and entered a deep cave, where a number of Japanese civilians had taken refuge along with a number of soldiers. He persuaded the Japanese to surrender, rather than die in the cave, and thus saved hundreds of lives.

There were other distinguished men in the Nisei military ranks. John Aiso became a lieutenant colonel on General MacArthur's staff. Sergeant Ben Kuroki of the Air Force flew fifty-eight missions, including the dreadful one over the Ploesti, Romania, oil fields, in which many planes were lost.

The war brought a considerable slackening of prejudice, and much of the credit for it must go to the Nisei soldiers and other servicemen. By 1943 the racial hysteria was quieting, and the Japanese found that at least some of them could "relocate"—that is, leave the camps if they wished to live in areas outside the Paciffc states.

Sometimes the racial slurs of the past were replaced by generous gestures. When the San Luis Obispo *Tribune-Telegram* published a picture of a Nisei soldier on its front page and racists objected, the newspaper put the objectors down firmly. "T-4 Higachi was good enough for the United States Army. . . . That makes him good enough for our front page."

When a little Japanese boy in New York woke up one morning to find that vandals had destroyed his victory garden, Occidentals rallied around to comfort him and replant it.

Japanese-Americans found, too, that jobs were opening up in the Midwest, as the nation felt the labor shortage caused by having so many men in uniform.

Japanese-Americans moved to Cleveland, Chicago, and New Jersey, places that had only been names to them before. They prospered there, and they found the bars of prejudice lowered. They made Occidental friends and Negro friends, whereas on the West Coast most Japanese had stuck to themselves.

It was not all easy sailing, of course. When 2,300 Japanese relocated in Colorado, some racists started a cry against them, and a move was made to deny aliens the right to own property in Colorado. But it failed when the people voted on the issue.

Someone in Missouri tried to introduce a measure to prohibit Japanese-American doctors from working in state institutions. The legislature voted it down. Some citizen of Ogden, Utah, tried to deny business licenses to Japanese. The United States courts knocked that out.

Around 80,000 Japanese-Americans remained in the concentration camps; but 36,000 did not, and they scattered across the country to give Americans in the length and breadth of the land acquaintance with people who were a little bit different. Almost uniformly the relocation was successful, and Occidental Americans began to learn a new tolerance toward Oriental peoples.

Yuri Katai, now a teen-ager, was one of those who left the camps. She decided she would go to Minnesota, where there was a chance to work in domestic service. She got a job with two other girls in the home of a wealthy judge, and the Caucasians were very nice to them. But Yuri was homesick, even for Gila River, and she spent hours writing letters back home to her family in the concentration camp.

Chapter Seven

The Nisei and Integration

Nowhere is the power of the American press indicated better than in a poll conducted by the Los Angeles *Times* at the end of 1943. The *Times* questioners discovered that its readers favored the exclusion of Japanese-Americans from the Pacific Coast by a margin of ten to one. Meanwhile, a Gallop poll of all five Western states showed that more than half the people would allow the Japanese-Americans to return to their homes. The conclusion must be that the *Times'* readers had been bombarded with so much anti-Japanese propaganda that they reacted to it.

Generally, the situation of the Japanese in America was improving, but dark spots still existed. Organized labor was opposed to the Japanese-Americans, particularly the old-fashioned American Federation of Labor. The newer, more class-conscious Congress of Industrial Organizations generally took a different view, and such unions as Harry Bridges'

I.L.W.U. the longshoremen's union, took in Japanese-Americans without prejudice. There were rallies and meetings and statements by racial groups opposing the return of the Japanese. A good amount of the opposition was admittedly by people who did not want the competition of Japanese farmers and truck gardeners.

There were voices of sanity. The Japanese had a newspaper, *Pacific Citizen,* edited by Larry Tajiri, a Nisei, and it dug into facts and reported on the propaganda, good and bad. Pearl Buck, the Nobel Prize-winning author, warned of the disaster of discrimination. She explained time and again how the discriminatory laws against the Japanese had helped bring about the Pacific war. The Japanese pro-Western liberal movement, she said, had been destroyed because of popular feeling against America's repressive actions against Japanese-Americans.

In a way, the tide began turning in 1944. Author Wallace Stegner published *One Nation,* a book that portrayed the Japanese sympathetically. Carey McWilliams published *Prejudice,* the story of the anti-Japanese movement and the internment. The liberal magazines *The Nation* and *The New Republic* led in the criticism of the policy. Many public figures came out for the Japanese.

In the early months of the war, the American Legion had been very strongly anti-Japanese-American, but as the Nisei went to war and fought so nobly, the Legion's position began to change. By the summer of 1944 Secretary of the Interior Harold Ickes was arguing with President Roosevelt for a basic change in policy, and Roosevelt resisted it only because he feared the reaction of the general public. He wanted to bring the Japanese-Americans back quietly and gradually to prevent any outcries.

One major effort in behalf of the Japanese-Americans was made by the American Civil Liberties Union. This organization had long before dedicated itself to the preservation of the freedom of all the people of America, and it fought for the Japanese. Its major weapon was the courts; the A.C.L.U. filed a number of suits to challenge the actions of government authorities in keeping the Japanese-Americans away from their homes. By 1944, when two of these suits were in progress, the direction of the war was quite apparent. The Japanese were being beaten badly, and there was no conceivable threat to the West Coast of the United States. There was very little reason to prevent the Japanese-Americans from returning to their places of residence—except the emotions of some racists and the greed of some others.

Among the cases handled by the A.C.L.U. was that of Missue Endo, a young stenographer with the California Highway Commission, who sued because she was deprived of her rights as a civil servant. The case was decided by the United State Supreme Court, which declared that loyal American citizens could not be detained by the government indefinitely.

Slowly, in the fall of 1944 the Japanese-Americans began to receive permission to go home again. In January, 1945, most of them were freed.

There were some incidents. Racists tried to burn down the barn of farmer Sumio Doi. The issue was clearly stated by a group of citizens of Placer County in northern California: The fruit growers did not want the Japanese competitors back. The big packers did want them back, however, because they were efficient farmers. In the Doi case the racists who tried to burn the barn were caught and prosecuted, but they were acquitted, despite the evidence.

There were incidents in other places as well. In Hood River, Oregon, the local American Legion Post removed the names of sixteen Nisei servicemen from their Roll of Honor. The outcry reached the national press, and *Collier's* magazine called it "blind hatred." The controversy lasted six weeks, then National Legion Commander Edward N. Scheiberling ordered that the names be replaced. Hood River was a heavily racist area, and the Japanese had a good deal of trouble there. But things began to happen: Caucasian Americans talked of boycotting Hood River apples in such places as Chicago and Cleveland—the big markets. A Portland banker began withholding credit from racists.

Some of the returning Japanese-Americans found their property damaged. Some found it intact. Some were harried by gunfire and incidents of racial violence; some were not bothered at all. What was most disturbing was that when racists were caught and prosecuted, they were almost always let off without punishment.

In the beginning of his term in office, California Governor Earl Warren acted with the racists most of the time, but in 1944 he began to have a change of heart. He was particularly distressed by the flouting of the law by irresponsible persons, and he began working to help better race relations.

As the Japanese-Americans came back to the cities of the West Coast, the pattern of their lives changed. Before the war they had lived in the Fillmore district of San Francisco, but when they came back in 1945, they discovered that the area had been filled up with blacks and others who had come to work in the shipyards during their absence. So the Japanese-Americans spread throughout the city. Some had difficulty because they had left possessions with friends who refused to return them. Others found that the basements and storehouses where they had kept their possessions had been burglarized. Some had no trouble at all.

The Japanese-Americans came home at a time when the United States was suffering a severe labor shortage, so the basic problem in the cities, that of competition for jobs, did not appear to bother them. Some skilled persons, such as physicians and nurses, found they were not welcome in the hospitals, and labor unions did not always behave themselves either. Such prejudice still seemed inevitable. In San Francisco machinists of Local 1305 of the Machinists Union stopped work in a bus barn when a Nisei was hired and reported for work. Mayor Roger Lapham of San Francisco made a personal appeal to stop the strike, and it did stop. Of such little bits and pieces were the threads of integration woven.

Labor was learning, if slowly, that the Japanese had rights like themselves. Some unions, notably the Teamsters, continued to cause trouble, but the C.I.O. was much better, and even the A.F. of L. began to break down its racial bars. The Fish Cannery Workers and the Fisherman's Union welcomed the Japanese back as if they had not been gone. It was not until several months after the war that Japanese were allowed to go near the waterfronts, but by the beginning of 1946 all that had ended.

Everywhere the Japanese came back either to try to pick up the threads of their old lives or to make new lives for themselves. There were still some difficulties. The city of Portland refused to issue business licenses to Japanese nationals—that is, to citizens of Japan. These Issei also found themselves in difficulty in other states, for the animosity against Japan itself was slower to die than that against the young Nisei, who had shown themselves to be such good Americans.

Even before the war ended, the opposition to the Japanese-Americans had tapered down to the hard core of the racists. There were incidents, but they were countered for the most part. San Francisco was under consideration as a site for the permanent home of the United Nations; but just as the United Nations conference met there, night raiders attacked a Japanese home in the area, and many delegates turned against San Francisco. This was duly noted by the daily press, which had become considerably more liberal in its racial views in the past few years.

By the spring of 1946 all relocation camps were closed, and

the Nisei were settling down. Half the Japanese-Americans had come back to the West Coast. More would come. Others were relocating in other parts of the United States for one reason or another. Slowly the restrictive laws and social practices began to break down.

The Nisei soldier had a good deal to do with some of the changes. The American Legion found itself embarrassed when it discovered posts that discriminated against soldiers who had won medals for valor, and when the Veterans of Foreign Wars and the American Veterans Committee proved more liberal, the Legion began to change.

By 1952 the restrictive laws against naturalization of persons born in Japan were removed, and some of the Issei became citizens of the United States. Some states where Japanese had been forbidden to own land began to change those restrictive laws. Japanese who had been deprived of property began to make claims and to receive awards. They usually did not get the full value of their claims, but they got something in most cases.

The old immigration laws were changed, and the provisions under which Orientals entered the United States were liberalized. These new regulations were far from perfect; they still discriminated against Orientals to some degree; but they were a huge improvement over the past.

Then came a number of other battles, such as those against restrictive real-estate covenants. For example, Bill Hosokawa, Sunday editor of the Denver *Post,* created a furor in the conservative Park Hill district of Denver when he proposed to buy a house there. Friends came to his support, and the racists of Park Hill were put down.

Hosokawa's whole postwar life story was an indication of the better conditions in which the Japanese-Americans were able to live. He joined the Denver *Post* shortly after the war and became assistant Sunday editor. He was competent, cheerful, and well liked by all the staff. He progressed to become

Sunday editor and then to become associate editor of the newspaper, after serving several stints as foreign correspondent, traveling to Japan, Vietnam, and other areas of Asia. Before the war the Denver *Post* had been as racist a newspaper as there was in the United States. After the war it not only employed Bill Hosokawa, but Larry Tajiri, the former editor of the *Pacific Citizen,* who became book critic for the *Post,* and several other Japanese-Americans.

The immigration laws of the United States were far from perfect in the 1950's and 1960's. The problem in that period was the prosperity of the United States compared to the general poverty of Asian countries. Consequently, had the gates been totally opened, serious dislocation problems would have arisen. Asians who were used to lower standards of living would have begun competing with American workers, and the result might have been a new wave of racism.

Imperfect as the laws were, they did allow the immigration of thousands of Japanese to America. From 1957 to 1966 visas were issued to 45,000 Japanese for immigration purposes. Many of these people had relatives already in the United States. Others, most wanted by the government, were scientists and specialists. Way down on the list were the common laborers, whose entrance had to be approved by the Department of Labor. But there was no *racial* discrimination in these laws. The Japanese were admitted on a quota system just like Spaniards, Greeks, or people from any other country.

As time went on, the Japanese moved more and more into the general framework of American life. William Muritani, a Nisei, became the first Japanese-American to argue cases before the United States Supreme Court. He was far from the last. Over the next few years some five hundred laws discriminating against Japanese-Americans were removed from the American statute books.

By the middle of the 1960's one could say truly that the age of racial discrimination against the Japanese had ended. The war brides brought home by Occidental and black servicemen melded into the communities of America. The many girls that Americans married during the Korean War did so, too. By the 1960's the sight of Japanese-Americans shopping in any grocery store in America did not even raise an eyebrow; it had become much too common.

As the scars of war faded and the Japanese began to prosper in Asia and to trade with America, increasing numbers of Japanese came to the United States to visit. In the late 1950's the Takashimaya Department Store, a truly Japanese store with its parent firm in Tokyo, was opened on Fifth Avenue in New York City. Japanese restaurants sprang up in cities across the American landscape, and they prospered because so many Americans had been to Japan that Japanese food and Japanese customs were no longer strange to them.

In many cities the Japanese-Americans live in developments and on quiet streets with Occidental neighbors. In Los Angeles, Little Tokyo still exists, a bustling small Japanese-American town, but at night the shop owners go home to houses in the suburbs. There is no longer a ghetto. To a large extent, the Japanese do congregate in certain suburbs of Los Angeles, but this is by choice and not because of any forced segregation or discriminatory laws. The same is true in San Francisco and in other cities.

Some people of Occidental birth still disliked the Japanese in the early 1970's, and some American military leaders predicted that in twenty-five years the United States would once again be at war with Japan. But the level of tolerance of Occidental Americans for Japanese-Americans was so great in 1973 that there could scarcely be any comparison with the conditions of thirty years earlier.

The old miscegenation laws had become silly with the return of Occidental Americans with their Japanese brides and with the general growth of racial tolerance and racial acceptance among the young. In earlier years miscegenation laws had been invoked to try to stop Occidental-Oriental marriages; by the middle of the 1960's these laws were declared unconstitutional by the United States Supreme Court in the Loving Case, which involved a Caucasian and his half black, half Indian wife. The case was argued by Nisei lawyer William Muritani.

So it could be said that by the early 1970's the Japanese-Americans had gained almost full American citizenship, if not quite full. There was still some residue of feeling in parts of the West, most of it either directly or indirectly engendered by economics and greed. There were still a few racists, a very few, but most of them were of the older generation. The Japanese-American dream was coming true.

Chapter Eight

Chinatown Revisited

Until the 1920's the Chinese community in the United States continued as a bachelor society because the immigration law and the cold reception the Chinese received made it virtually impossible for these Orientals to settle down.

Family life in Chinese America began with the small merchant class, and the reason for this was that "merchants" were exempted from the exclusion acts and so could bring in families and wives. Sometimes merchants could be persuaded by restaurant owners and others who were excluded to list their families as part of the merchant's family. Except for the six years when the immigration law of 1924 was in effect, the Chinese segment of America slowly began to grow.

The emergence of family life in the Chinese community led to the decline of the tongs. The working day for family businesses was long, and the whole family worked. There was little time for meetings or gossip in the streets. A child grew up in the family business. If it was a laundry, the little boy or girl would begin at the age of four or five to fold towels and handkerchiefs. When he or she was eight or nine years old, the tasks became more complicated. There were big pressing machines to run and shirts to iron and the counter to tend. The children were very valuable because in public school they achieved a much greater command of English than their parents usually had. As they reached high-school age they were able to help with the complicated machinery of American business, tax forms and licenses, and they were able to deal with the outside, or Occidental, world.

These were happy families in spite of their hard work and poverty. Everyone cooperated. The older children took care of the younger ones, and they were all taught from an early age the Confucian principle of subordination of self to the family principle. But that did not mean great sacrifice or unhappiness.

One American Chinese who grew up in this period was Jade Snow Wong, whose home was Chinatown in San Francisco. Her father came to the United States early in the 1900's as an accountant to audit the books of the San Francisco branch of his Chinese trading firm. He stayed on to become a Presbyterian minister, then returned to China, and because he was a professional man, was allowed to bring his wife and children to America.

Jade Snow's mother came to America with feet only 2½ inches long. They had been bound in the Chinese fashion when she was a baby, and they had never grown. But the Reverend Mr. Wong warned his wife not to bind their daughters' feet, because America had different customs. So the five little Wong girls were saved this torture.

Back in America Mr. Wong went into a family business to support his growing family. That meant his wife worked at the shop all day every day, and the children had to take care of each other. Jade Snow did most of the family's laundry in big galvanized buckets in the bathroom. She also dusted, swept, and cleaned the stove. One night a week her mother stayed up late and did the floor mopping and the heavy tasks.

For her work around the house, Jade Snow earned fifty cents a week, and by cleaning her big brother's room and doing other chores, she managed to earn a total of about three dollars a month. That was her "spending money." She grew up to expect nothing but the necessities from her family. If she wanted luxuries, she had to earn them.

Mrs. Wong's one luxury was the "foreign movies." On Saturday nights she left the shop and took the children to the neighborhood theater, where they saw a serial, a double feature, a cartoon, and a newsreel. Their favorites were Tarzan pictures and Westerns. After the movies they went home and read the Sunday papers. Jade Snow, Jade Precious Stone, and Forgiveness always read "Dick Tracy," "Bringing Up Father," and the "Katzenjammer Kids."

On Sunday, since theirs was a Christian family, they had breakfast and then studied the Sunday-school lesson. Jade Snow would translate it from English into Chinese, thus accomplishing two ends. Then it was time for Sunday school, where they were taught by an Occidental lady. Church, which was conducted in Chinese, followed, and then came lunch. Jade Snow's father did not come home for lunch on Sunday because he was treasurer of the church and had to attend to business affairs.

After lunch Mrs. Wong and the children went for a Sunday walk along Grant Avenue, past the Chinese grocery stores and the shops in their tiled buildings with pagoda-style roofs. Sunday was usually the day for Chinese funerals, and so they often had a colorful procession to watch. If it was a Christian burial, it would be done in the Christian way; but if the dead man was an old believer, the mourners always dressed in white, and professional wailers accompanied the body to the grave site, crying and moaning all the way.

Jade Snow Wong liked the contrast between the Chinese grocery shops, with their *bok choy,* hanging sausages, wine-flavored ducks, and fresh ginger, and the delicatessens found in the Italian district of North Beach, just a few steps from Chinatown, with their hanging cheeses, salamis, and good-smelling bread. She also enjoyed going down to Fisherman's Wharf, with its awnings, boats, seafood restaurants, and automobiles, and mingling there with the ladies from Nob Hill, who did not know a piece of *bok choy* from a piece of *tofu.* (*Bok choy* is Chinese cabbage. *Tofu* is bean curd, the Chinese substitute for milk in many ways.)

Grammar school in San Francisco's Chinatown was the Commodore Stockton Public School, which was almost entirely Chinese in makeup. At the junior high-school level, the children moved on to a mixed school, but for two hours a day nearly every Chinese youth also attended a Chinese school. Here the children were supposed to learn the Chinese language, history, and culture, but with most of these young Chinese-Americans, interest in things Chinese waned as they moved into high school. There they began to act almost exactly like Occidental teen-agers. They wanted "sharp" clothes, cars, and "a girl."

From here on in their lives, the cultural differences of the generations became acute. The old family people had been married by arrangement, which was the Chinese custom. The young people wanted romance and courtship and the right to choose their own mates. Parents wanted their children to prosper, and in the 1930's they could enter various colleges, really for the first time.

But here again was the rub. Once they had graduated as teachers or accountants, very seldom was there a job for Chinese-Americans outside Chinatown. So many of these youths had to face a knotty question: Did their future lie in America or in China? Their background, for the most part, was far more American than Chinese, but their continued rejection by Americans of Occidental birth was their most serious problem.

One such youth was James Low, whose father was a garment worker in Chinatown. James went to Commodore Stockton Grammar School and then to Francisco Junior High School and Galileo High School. The greatest influence on him was the teachers in the Chinese schools, who often flavored their lessons with Chinese politics. James Low grew up during the crisis period of Chinese history. He was born in 1925. Six years later came the Mukden Incident and the Japanese seizure of Manchuria. Then came more humiliation by the Japanese, and his teachers discussed it nearly every day.

James Low was not quite sure what he was going to do with his life. Growing up during the Depression years, he saw that opportunities for Chinese in America seemed quite limited. His father was completely disillusioned, and he pointed out the experience of a man who had trained to be a mining engineer and ended up running a garment factory because he could not get work in his field or virtually no work outside the Chinese community.

Nevertheless, James Low went on to the University of California at Berkeley and became an engineer himslf. One day in San Francisco he met a girl who had come from China. He courted her in the usual American way, and they wanted to get married. Her parents objected strenuously. She was from the Chungshan district of Kwangtung Province, but his family came from the Namhoi district.

Why, asked the girl's family, was she marrying someone from so far away?

He was not from far away, she said. He lived on Jackson Street, and they lived on Montgomery Street.

Here was a glimpse of the tremendous difference between

the generations. The girl had become Americanized in her few years in San Francisco, and in spite of family objections, she and James Low were married.

The Pacific war brought about a great change in Chinatown, U.S.A., and in the relationships between Chinese-Americans and Occidentals. As the Japanese grew more aggressive in Asia and American concern in Washington grew, American friendship for China reasserted itself. The last year or so of the 1930's and the beginning of the 1940's brought real encouragement to the young Chinese-Americans. For the first time, one of them said later, he felt that he and his friends had a chance to make it in American society.

As the war in China grew worse, even before Pearl Harbor, Madame Chiang Kai-shek, who had been educated at Wellesley College, came to America and received huge acclaim. Occidentals began raising money for Chinese war relief, and the United States government began assisting Chiang Kai-shek's government.

In Chinatown, U.S.A., Chiang was never totally popular. Many of the people believed he did not fight the Japanese hard enough, that he was more concerned with wielding the instruments of power than with saving China from its enemies. But the Chinese-Americans responded gladly to the Occidental interest and sympathy, which created new jobs and new chances for them in the general society.

With the war the opening of shipyards and war industries brought more opportunities. There was a shortage of workers, so there were no more complaints from labor about the "heathen Chinee" stealing bread from the mouth of the Irish-American, the German-American, or the Italian-American.

Chinese-Americans served as valiantly in the war as did their Japanese counterparts, although they were not given either the same opportunities for valor as the Japanese or the same publicity. On the other hand, though, they did not have the same degree of animosity to overcome, for the war itself solved most of their problems.

By and large, the Chinese of America supported the Nationalist government and the Kuomintang party of Chiang Kai-shek, although in some cases they were very critical of the state of affairs in China in the second quarter of the twentieth century.

Like Sun Yat-sen, Chiang had sought support from the overseas Chinese, or Hua Ch'iao. In 1937 a Kuomintang representative named Dip Lum came to San Francisco to represent the Nationalists and to raise funds to support the war. At first he was successful because events in China had forced at least a temporary alliance between Chiang and the Chinese Communists of Mao Tse-tung. Lum was a very skillful politician, and he obtained the support of important figures in the Six Companies, the family associations, and the tongs. So the ties between the Kuomintang and the Chinese of America seemed quite secure.

The Establishment in the Chinese community was very much in favor of the Nationalist government. This was important because the Six Companies had really been the government of Chinatown since the 1880's. This superorganization controlled the Chinese Central High School and the Chinese hospital. The fifty-five members of the board of directors of the Six Companies had an interlocking directorate of all the important organizations in San Francisco's Chinatown. This city, of course, was the center of Chinese life in America.

That control was used indirectly, usually. For example, the land of Chinatown consisted of many small parcels, 65 percent of them controlled by various family associations. The men of the Six Companies represented the family associations. Through business and personal connections, these men were able to control the economic life of the community and to suppress newspapers and other voices of dissent. Sometimes they did so. The local Chinese-language newspapers almost always supported the Six Companies' views on public affairs.

After the war younger men and sometimes even women began to challenge the old order of things. And there were many other changes. Young Chinese veterans, back from the war, insisted on and got their rights. The old restrictive covenants broke down in 1947, and after that the Chinese could live anywhere. More important, for the most part they were welcome almost everywhere—the old racial intolerance was dying.

The Chinatown of the 1940's became a different city. The young second-generation Chinese moved out. They still came back to shop, to see friends, and to feel the way of life of Chinatown, but they lived elsewhere. The old people remained, to be joined by the many refugees and by others who simply sought the United States as a place to live at the end of World War II. Many of these people came to America speaking no English, and so Chinatown was their refuge, a place where they could find an atmosphere most like the old homeland.

The businesses continued. The restaurants prospered as Occidental Americans came to indulge their newly acquired taste for Oriental foods, and as tourists began to flock to San Francisco from the rest of the nation and abroad. With an immigration quota ever going up, although slowly, Chinatown changed. Indeed, the change was apparent immediately after World War II.

Chapter Nine

The Indian Exodus

During his years in India, Mahatma Gandhi brought his scheme of Satyagraha, or nonviolence, to a pitch that so attracted the Indian people in the end that he became their undisputed leader in the struggle against British colonialism.

But in retrospect Gandhi and his followers decided that the influence he had exerted in South Africa was largely due to a basically humane group of men in power in the British colonies there. This conclusion was the result of experience with a new group of white leaders in Africa, who were determined to maintain white dominance at any price.

South Africa is hardly regarded as part of the Western world geographically, but thc British and the Boers there certainly brought Western traditions and culture. In practice, the isolation of the three million whites and their knowledge that they were surrounded by eighteen million nonwhites led the British and Boers to adopt repressive measures to maintain their superiority.

According to projections, the population of South Africa in the year 2000 will include six million whites and thirty million nonwhites. This understanding became the basis for the white minority's national policy, and by 1970 the rulers who developed from it had brought about the highest execution rate and the highest rate of political punishment and imprisonment in the world. In such a climate it was hard to see how Satyagraha or any other peaceful policy by the Indians could succeed. The Gandhi legacy was victim of this repression as much as any other way of life.

During his stay in South Africa, Gandhi established fifteen miles northeast of Durban a farm called Phoenix, which was successful both as a farm and as a social project. It became a center of Indian activity and planning.

After Gandhi left in the early years of the twentieth century, his second son, Manilal Gandhi, stayed on to lead the Indians of South Africa. He became the editor of *Indian Opinion,* the magazine through which the Indian population aired its views and acquainted whites with Indian doings and Indian ideas. In 1951 his wife, Mrs. Manilal Sushila Gandhi, started a school for Indians and black children at the Phoenix center, but unfortunately, in the years after Gandhi left Africa, the South African government cracked down on all but whites. The school could not succeed in the face of such repressive policies.

In the early 1970's, spurred by the need for trade, the South African government went through some ridiculous circumlocutions in racial matters. For example, since there were only a few hundred Japanese in South Africa, they were declared "honorary whites," and they have white status except for one caveat: They cannot intermarry with Occidentals.

The Chinese were often lumped with the Indians as Asiatics, but not always. The status of the Chinese in the early 1970's was still indeterminate, but with the growing power of the People's Republic of China, it seemed quite probable that the Chinese would soon be getting better treatment and a new status in South Africa. For one reason, since there were only nine thousand Chinese in South Africa in 1970, they could hardly be called a serious economic threat, and in that country, as elsewhere, racial intolerance is basically an economic matter.

The modern history of South African racism dates back to 1910, when four colonies, Transvaal, Cape, Orange Free State, and Natal, joined to form the Union of South Africa. In the next few years the colonies worked to combine their ideas and policies. At first, the nonwhites in the Cape Province were protected by law. It has often been said, and only half jokingly, that the British won the Boer War, but the Boers won South Africa, because in the years after World War I, the enlightened politics of Cecil Rhodes, the father of South Africa, began to erode away, and much sterner attitudes began to prevail. General Smuts, Gandhi's old antagonist, became the leading figure of the land, and in those interim years he ruled as prime minister a good deal of the time.

For years Smuts walked a narrow line and kept power, but after World War II his United party was defeated by the racist Nationalist party. South Africa then began to undergo rapid change, and in a direction that shocked the rest of the world.

The election of 1948 sealed the modern fate of South Africa and the Asians and nonwhite peoples who lived there. The Nationalist party ran on a platform of apartheid, or complete separation of the races. The Nationalists secured a small majority of seats in the Parliament and then began unashamedly to put into effect their policy of racism. Dr. Daniel Malan, prime minister, established three classes of citizens.

First was the white class, which was to be dominant. Second were the "coloreds," which meant everyone who was neither white nor black. It included some two million people who were the products of various mixed marriages and some six hundred thousand Asians, most of them from various parts of India and Pakistan. The third group consisted of the blacks.

The black man's position in South Africa is dreadful and seems almost hopeless, barring revolution. The position of the Asians is better, but not that much better. The black man is needed to do the white man's labor. The Asian occupies a more middle ground, but he still does not have the full rights of citizenship or anything close to such rights.

Many Asians said, and still say, as did Gandhi's friend Abdallah Sheth, that the Indians stay only because of the money they can make through their shrewdness as traders and businessmen. Now, three generations later, it is far more complicated than that. Many Asians have returned to Indian states where their parents were born or their grandparents once lived and found that the life there was so foreign to their own that only the language served as a tie. For better or worse, in the last half of the twentieth century, most of these Asians are South Africans, and they have as much claim to the name as the Boers or the Anglicans.

But right*s*—that is another matter.

In 1948 the Malan government began moves to cut off all coloreds from the vote. After a long argument in Parliament, the members of the government compromised on a measure that violated the South African constitution but was acceptable to the majority of whites. The coloreds would vote on a separate list and would have the right to elect four whites to represent their interests in Parliament. This law was passed in 1956.

Also in this period the whites began to tighten old restrictions and to make new ones against any kind of integration, social or otherwise. Indians and other nonwhites must go to separate counters at the post office to buy stamps. In railroad stations they must go to separate counters to buy tickets. They cannot use white washrooms in most establishments, and they cannot try on clothes in department stores, although they are allowed to buy the clothes on a guesswork basis.

In 1949 mixed marriages were prohibited "to promote racial purity." In 1950 severe penalties were invoked against both whites and nonwhites if they were caught indulging in sexual intercourse with members of other races.

In 1950 the Population Registration Act was passed, and that did to all South Africa what Gandhi had once fought against so valiantly in the Transvaal. Then the policy of racial segregation became even stronger. All Asians must carry identity cards, since they are classified as coloreds. They have separate and unequal schools, better than those of the blacks, but not nearly so good as those of the whites.

In education, students of all races had been admitted to the schools until the racist policies became the law. Then the nonwhites were gradually pushed out. In 1961 Witwatersrand University had 258 nonwhite students, some of them Asians; in 1964 there were only 11.

The laws are arbitrary, and they reflect the economic considerations very strongly. In some areas an Indian can drive a truck, but only a truck of a certain weight. Heavy trucking is a privilege reserved for whites, for that is where the most money can be earned. Asians and coloreds of the African-white mixture are very seldom allowed to learn skilled trades. These are reserved for the whites. Once again the selfishness of the white laboring class in racial relations seems even stronger than that of the upper class.

Late in the 1960's the apartheid policy was still being perfected in detail. A Coloured Representative Council was established to manage the Department of Coloured Affairs. Then a special Department of Indian Affairs was established to manage the Indians, and a National Indian Council consisting of twenty-one Indians was created to act as a go-between with the government. It seemed likely that the Indians would have more say in the management of their own affairs in the 1970's, but this was a far cry from full citizenship.

Long before the final breakup of the British Empire, the Indian government became the most vocal enemy of the South African government. Indian prime ministers have fought the Africans tooth and nail in every conceivable way, from the Empire councils to the United Nations, but their enmity has done little to better the lot of the Indians in South Africa. They are tolerated there only because of their wealth and because of their number. They are businessmen by and large, and South Africa would suffer badly if somehow it suddenly contrived to get rid of them. This is at once the salvation and the difficulty of the Indians. They have too much at stake to pull out and too little power to exert influence. In a land where the governing power is dedicated to racism, they sit and wait.

Many of the Indians' attempts to better the country are met with rejection. Mrs. Gandhi's school was one of them. When the South African government began the apartheid policy in earnest, it was declared illegal for Mrs. Gandhi to teach both Asians and the black-white coloreds, to say nothing of blacks, so all but the Asians were forced out. Later the school was taken over by the government Department of Indian Affairs.

The race policies of South Africa work the same way the old American policies used to work against the Chinese and Japanese. Mrs. Gandhi's son went to India for a visit, and while there he married an Indian girl. The South African government would allow him to return, but would not let his wife come to South Africa to live. So young Gandhi remained in India.

The magazine *Indian Opinion* did not last long after Manilal Gandhi's death, either. It closed down in 1961. By that time Mrs. Gandhi was beginning to lose heart, and she considered moving to India herself, as other Asians of South Africa were doing. But she was persuaded by her daughter and son-in-law, Ela and Mewa Ramgobin, to remain on at Phoenix, and there, with much outside help, they created a clinic. Soon they were treating fifteen hundred patients a month, most of them Africans.

They stayed on in South Africa to wait for a better day, when Asians might achieve full citizenship. But could it be so? The experience of Indians in other parts of Africa indicated that the going was bound to be rough, even if the South Africans changed their whole policy, or if one day the blacks rose up in successful rebellion.

The case of the Indians in Uganda is an example of the worst that might happen in a new society. Beginning in the early days of European colonization of East Africa, when the British, Germans, and Portuguese vied for power and influence, Britain had encouraged Indians to come to East Africa from their homeland. The Indians were a civilized people, part of the British Empire, and through them the British hoped to increase their influence. The Indians were able to deal with the local people, Arabs and blacks, on a level that the British could not, for part of the mystique of the Empire lay in maintaining the myth of superiority.

The society of East Africa developed along three layers, with the British as the lords and masters at the top, the blacks at the bottom of the heap, and the Indians as the merchants and middlemen and middle class in between. Zanzibar, the island off the coast of Africa, was soon dominated by Indians and Indian trade. The Indians moved into Kenya and Uganda, other areas of British control, after the whole of East Africa was taken from the Germans in 1918. By mid-century some 300,000 Indians and Pakistanis were living in East Africa. As the British built railroads, they brought in Asian laborers, and many of them stayed on.

But these Asians did not mix in with the black population. They kept to themselves, and they were encouraged to do this by the British. They became policemen, shopkeepers, accountants, and civil servants. They never received more than the barest respect from the British and few enough rewards. They had an abiding dislike of the African blacks, and the blacks felt that these Asian foreigners had somehow contrived with the British to exploit them. As black nationalism grew, so did antipathy to the Asians, even though many Asian merchants and traders befriended the blacks.

The emerging black states pondered what they might do with the Asians. Many of these Indians and Pakistanis held British passports and chose to retain their British citizenship when the question of nationality arose. Among themselves they spoke any of several Asian languages such as Gujarati. They did not really mix into the African scene, nor did they wish to. If they had an image of a proper society, it was, unfortunately, almost precisely a British image. They had been uprooted from India when India was a British colony, and they had not shared with the Asians of India the pains and pleasures of nationalism.

The British had kept the Asians off the land in most parts of East Africa. Thus they had congregated in the towns and cities. When the black governments came in, they continued the policy of keeping the Asians off the land. In 1968 Kenya inaugurated the work permit, which enabled Indians and other foreigners to hold jobs. There was, obviously, a good deal of opportunity for speculation and influence peddling in the work permit situation, and it became scandalous to a degree. But by and large the government of Jomo Kenyatta in Kenya was enlightened enough to understand that the Indians were still needed as traders and merchants, professionals, and middle management officials.

There was some discomfort, causing some Asians to go

home, but by the 1970's it seemed that the Asians would be able to mix into the developing Kenyan society, if they so chose. The acting chief justice—head of the judicial system—was a Kenyan of Indian descent. So was one judge of the Industrial Court of Appeals. The Asians were far more than merely tolerated. "Integration," as the word is used in America, however, was something else again and would be for a good long time in East Africa.

Affairs took quite a different path in Uganda after General Idi Amin took power. President Milton Obote had in 1969 established trade-licensing and immigration restrictions on Asians, but the Asians had been left largely alone, particularly the merchants and other businessmen. In 1972, the year after Amin took over, he announced that the Asians who were citizens of Great Britain, India, Pakistan, and Bangladesh would be expelled from Uganda, and in very short order. This was partly a spasm of super–black nationalism, but there was more to it than that. In Uganda, more than in Kenya, the Indians and Pakistanis had rejected the concept of mingling with the blacks, and here was the source of much irritation to the emerging black leaders. Some of them felt that the Indians had no interest in the land except to exploit the blacks to their own advantage. Undoubtedly, there was a truth behind this charge. The Asian habit of sticking very close to the small community of their language and place of origin added to the belief.

When the Amin government announced that the Asians were to be expelled almost immediately, the word created consternation among these people. Many of them decided to go to Great Britain itself, because over a period of time they had learned that opportunity of the kind they were used to having seldom existed on the Indian subcontinent. These Asians had cast their lot with what was in effect the Western world, and now they would follow that star to London.

The news that thousands of British-passport-holding Asians were about to descend on Britain was greeted in England with considerable consternation. Until World War II there had been virtually no color consciousness in Britain. British soldiers and sailors went abroad, as they had been doing for two hundred years. They came home talking of "wogs" (Wily Oriental Gentlemen) and generally feeling superior to the people of Asia. However, the Asians who came to Britain were not mistreated officially, and until they became so numerous as to endanger the workingmen, or their concept of themselves, there was no real prejudice. At the very highest levels, Asians were richer and often more cultured than their British peers. At the middle level, the barristers, students, and doctors were considered acceptable enough, as long as it was understood they were learning in England to practice abroad.

In the 1960's and 1970's Britain had her troubles, and among them was a heavy rash of immigration from West Indian islands and from the Orient. These immigrants were not playboys or students or vacationers, but people who came to seek jobs and a livelihood on England's shores. Naturally, they brought with them a new resentment of the old kind: They were an economic threat to the workingman.

West Indians had already moved into certain areas of the cities, and as their numbers grew in the schools and on the streets, so did the British workingmen's resentment. Added to that now came the Asians, and the resentment and fear grew keen.

The London *Daily Express,* which had always played the popular theme of the moment, began warning of the Oriental menace, much in the vein adopted by the San Francisco press more than seventy-five years earlier. Other popular newspapers took up the cry. A poll published by the *Express* indicated that only 6 percent of the British readers of that newspaper wanted the Asians from Uganda to come in at all. The

"Keep Britain White" movement, whose activities were reported in the popular press with gusto, began its efforts to restrict the immigration of Orientals and brown- and black-skinned peoples.

Just the same, thousands of the Ugandan Asians came to Britain in 1972, and Britain, by her own standards, was bound to take them.

One such family was that of Kantilal Rao. He and his wife and six of his children were soon living in Wembley, a suburb of London that had become a refuge for West Indians and Asians.

The Raos were very lucky in a way. When the cry came out against them and they had to move from the land of their adoption in such short time, their second daughter, Kundan, who was twenty years old, was already in London. She had gone to study the Montessori method of teaching, hoping to introduce it into Uganda. But, of course, that was all before the announcement of General Idi Amin.

Kundan Rao had saved about $400 while she was in Britain. She had been expecting to use it for a trip home to Uganda that year. Instead, she now rented a house for the family in the suburb of Kingsbury. It was all she could find, and it was very expensive—$84 a week. That was too expensive, as it turned out; but it gave the Raos a base, so that when they came in at Heathrow Airport, with eight suitcases, a handful of boxes, and $132, they could tell the customs and immigration men that they had a place to go and a relative who had some resources. Thus they escaped the misery and upset of living in one of the resettlement camps that were being set up in abandoned air and army bases around England and Wales.

Kantilal Rao had been brought to Uganda as an infant and he had grown up there. Uganda was his country. It was not the Uganda of General Amin, but the Uganda of the British Empire. Over the years Kantilal Rao had prospered there, in the fashion of the Indian middle class. He had gone into the travel business and become manager of the White Band Travel Service, Ltd., with its offices in the Grand Hotel in Kampala. In pre-Amin Uganda this was a very good job. Mr. Rao took home 4,800 Ugandan shillings each month, or $680, and that was an excellent income. The family lived well, and the children went to middle schools, where they played tennis and cricket and learned the ways of a British and colonial society.

Then suddenly that Uganda ceased to exist. It all ended in 1972, and the Raos were forced out of their comfortable home, their comfortable surroundings, and their middle-class way of life. They were uprooted, and they ended up in Heathrow Airport with a pitiful little collection of belongings, all they had to show for a lifetime in Uganda.

After four weeks in which Kantilal Rao scoured the newspapers and haunted the employment agencies looking for work in his own field, the Raos had to move to cheaper quarters. He could not find work that suited him. He had training as an accountant and as a travel man, but there were no openings. He went to the employment service one day, under the impression that there was an accounting job open, and found that what was wanted were sweepers and cleaners on the railroad. In India such was the work of the very lowest classes. Untouchables had been sweepers in the old days. Kantilal Rao recoiled from the prospect and flatly refused even to consider it. He was a professional, a white-collar man, and he was looking for white-collar work.

The trouble was that there were no such jobs for Ugandan Indians in the fall of 1972 in and around London. So Kantilal Rao stayed at home, reading the employment columns of the newspapers, checking various leads, and collecting the fifty-five dollars in unemployment benefits he received each week. The younger Raos found the transition easier.

The family had to move to a house on Thulby Road in Wembley, which they could afford. It was a run-down district, a workingman's district, and it was, it appeared, turning Asian. Already most of the Indians and West Indians had moved into the Borough of Brent, which had a population of about 280,000, and there had been white repercussions against this new group of Asians from Uganda, particularly when they joined the applicants for low-income housing. Already some 7,500 had applied for this housing, and the whites feared that the government would give the Asians partiality and that they would be forced out. So alarmed did some whites become that they began issuing petitions to control Asian immigration. It was all very reminiscent of what happened in San Francisco in the 1870's.

Once settled in, the Raos had to live with their neighbors' resentment and find a new way of life. Kundan found a job in the telecommunications department of the Post Office. (Unlike the American Post Office Department, the British Post Office handles telegrams and cables.) She earned forty-four dollars a week, which she brought home to the family. The third daughter, Jayshree, who was eighteen, found a job as a cashier in a fish market. The three boys went to high school, two of them to the local school and one to Alperton School, a special institution established for the Ugandans. Seven-year-old Jiten went to the local grammar school, with other Asians, West Indians, and Occidental children. There was another daughter in her middle twenties, but she and her husband had emigrated to Canada. They would see her only for an occasional visit.

The Raos and some twenty-seven thousand other Ugandans had descended suddenly on England, and the problems were not going to be easy to solve. Some eighty-five hundred Ugandan Indians had gone back to India, but they indicated to others that it was not a good idea for many, unless they had strong ties and connections. Some had gone to Canada; a lucky one thousand had gone to the United States; and some had gone to Zambia and other countries.

In time the Raos will undoubtedly find a new way of life, although it is likely to be a comedown from the old one and remain so. The status of a middle-class Indian in British society is not what the status of that same person was in pre-nationalist African society. There were jobs for Asians in London in 1972, but most of them were menial work.

The story of Kantilal Rao was very much the story of the middle-aged men of his group. Britain had created this middle class in its Empire for the purposes of empire. Now these people were coming to Britain and finding the going very hard. There were by 1972 a million and a half Indians, Pakistanis, and West Indians in the British Isles, and the working people were aroused.

Chapter Ten

Hawaii: They Called It a Melting Pot

One great attribute of the Hawaiian Islands has been the almost total indifference with which the people who live there have viewed race. Only with the coming of statehood have the census takers used methods that concentrate on race. For the first time the race problems of the rest of the United States have intruded themselves on the Hawaiian consciousness. The race danger in Hawaii is that it will become more like the mainland, instead of the mainland becoming more like the islands.

As with nearly all Oriental migration to the West, immigration into Hawaii began in the middle of the nineteenth century. Before that time the independent Polynesian kingdom had allowed traders to come in, and many had. They were American, British, French, and Chinese for the most part. The Hawaiians called them all haole, or stranger, and paid no attention to their color. A Chinese was known from an

American largely because of his queue and black pantaloons and his dietary habits.

During the 1860's and early 1870's, Chinese laborers began coming to the islands to work on the plantations, but there were not very many of them until the late 1870's. Then in the single year 1883 four shiploads of immigrants arrived from Hong Kong. The Hawaiians were distressed, but not for the reason one might suppose. They simply did not like the idea of these people coming without wives or without obligations.

What had happened, obviously, was that some entrepreneur in Hong Kong, who had been promising laborers work in the United States, suddenly found himself cut off by the Exclusion Act. So he loaded his workers aboard ships anyhow and just dumped them, without jobs or contracts, on the Hawaiian Islands. Consequently, in 1884 Chinese were found to make up 22 percent of the Hawaiian population and half the foreign population.

But that was an anomaly. Most of the Chinese did not plan to stay, and as they acquired a little money in the fields, they went home. So the increase in the Chinese population was not very great, and the population steadily became a smaller percentage of the whole.

The Hawaiian imperial government was concerned in the last quarter of the nineteenth century about the dying out of the Hawaiian race and the increase in the number of foreigners in the islands. Not that the members of the government resented the foreigners, but they worried about the impact on their own people. Following the coming of Captain Cook in 1778, the Hawaiians had been ravaged by the diseases the whites brought with them: syphilis, tuberculosis, and bubonic plague. In this island paradise, the Polynesians had not had the hundreds of years of immunities built up by Westerners, and they died by the thousands. The original island population was somewhere around 300,000 Polynesians. By 1882 it was down to around 40,000, and King

Kalakaua was so concerned that he sent a special emissary to Japan asking the emperor to send people to Hawaii. Kalakaua believed that the Hawaiians and the Japanese sprang from the same racial stock, and he wanted to use Japanese blood to rejuvenate his kingdom.

But Kalakaua's ambassador was greeted coldly in Tokyo. The Japanese believed they were a holy people, related to no others, and the emperor sternly forbade anyone to emigrate to Hawaii. Consequently, all Kalakaua could attract, with all his offers, was 148 Japanese, who came away secretly in defiance of the emperor's orders.

Through strong pressure exerted by American planters and others, the Japanese imperial government was forced to change its position on emigration, and in 1886 Japanese movement to Hawaii began seriously. A Japanese could make the trip to Hawaii by steamer for sixty-seven dollars. He came with a contract as a laborer on a plantation. He had to pay back the sixty-seven dollars advanced by the contractor, but then he was on his own.

The planters and others found the Japanese most agreeable, at first. When the number of Japanese increased to the point where they became 22 percent of the population, the American businessmen who dominated the island began to worry. They began to import Portuguese workers instead of Orientals. So the Portuguese population also began to grow.

After the islands became a territory of the United States in 1900, the various exclusion acts cut into the immigration of Orientals to Hawaii. At that time the population was 154,000, of which the largest number by far were Japanese: 61,000. In retrospect, King Kalakaua seemed to have had his way after all, even though his kingdom was long gone. Hawaiians and part Hawaiians now made up only 40,000. There were 25,000 Chinese, about 18,000 Portuguese, and a virtual handful of mainland Americans and people from other lands.

Yet in keeping with American feeling, the fear of "Orientalization" of this new territory became the guiding principle for controlling immigration. The big stress among the Americans who owned property was to bring in Caucasians, to prevent the Orientals from "taking over." In 1905 the territorial legislature created a Board of Immigration, whose task was to encourage Occidentals and discourage Orientals. This board operated until the early days of World War I.

The Immigration Board brought in more Portuguese and some Russians, but after a few months most of these people were lured to the American Pacific Coast, where opportunities were greater and the way of life seemed more attractive. So the planters were faced with the old problem: Where could they find cheap labor?

The answer was to defy the growing Occidental opinion on the mainland and bring in more Japanese contract laborers. Between 1900 and 1910 seventy-seven thousand Japanese came to Hawaii. At the same time seventy-five thousand left, either to go to the mainland or to return to Japan. But eighteen thousand Japanese children were born in the islands, too.

Then came a new group, the Koreans. Some five thousand of them arrived, and for the most part, they stayed on, because Japan had taken over their homeland and made it a part of the Japanese Empire. The Occidentals who worried about Orientals kept on introducing Portuguese laborers and Puerto Ricans and even some Filipinos. As the feeling against the Japanese grew, the importation of Filipinos increased, until some 125,000 of them came to the islands.

Although these immigrants were brought mostly to work on the plantations, they gravitated toward the cities. Oahu gained by far the most population, with Honolulu becoming the largest city and remaining that way. The Chinese had headed for Honolulu for the most part, and the Koreans also went to the cities. The Portuguese remained on the plantations. The Japanese, too, tended to stay on the land. Yet there were so many of them in terms of the islands' population that the Japanese also became the dominant group in the cities. As on the mainland, however, many Japanese found land and began to work it for themselves. As always, they were good farmers and successful in their agriculture.

In the cities the various racial groups at first congregated in their own quarters, but there was never any so clearly defined area as Little Tokyo of Los Angeles or Chinatown of San Francisco.

The Chinese, with their strong mercantile sense, settled near Honolulu Harbor, and this area became known as Chinatown. Chinatown, Hawaii, did not last very long, however. In 1882, at the height of the anti-Chinese agitation on the mainlnd, the Chinese of the islands did group together, but that year was the high point of their concentration in Honolulu. Soon they began to move out, and by the middle of the twentieth century, there was only a trace of the old Chinatown, along Pauahi, Maunakea, and Smith streets. The Chinese population in the old Chinatown area had shrunk to 5 percent of the Chinese population in Honolulu.

The Japanese settled first in the Palama, River Street, and Kakaako districts, with the truck gardeners and animal raisers settling in the outlying areas. In the years that followed, more Japanese districts grew up, but the old ones declined. In modern times the major Japanese areas are the Moiliili-McCully and Palolo districts. The reason for the Japanese concentration, even though it is not heavy in terms of the total Japanese population, is the need for cultural facilities. Here they have their teahouses, Buddhist temples, Shinto shrines, and bathhouses.

The most important aspect of Hawaiian life is change. As the new immigrants improved their economic position in the islands, they moved. Most of them came to the slums, lived there awhile, and then moved to better districts. As they moved, the children began to press the parents to live according to the American way as seen in the magazines, in the movies, and later on television.

The Chinese, as the oldest Oriental inhabitants, moved out in some number to an area called the Bingham Tract during the 1920's. They built thoroughly American houses there and lived in the Western manner. As time went on, some of them moved on to more prestigious neighborhoods, in the American tradition of conspicuous wealth, and other nationalities moved into the Bingham Tract. By the 1970's the Bingham Tract was just another neighborhood, with a slightly higher proportion of Chinese than some others.

Occidentals, haoles, congregated at first in the Nuuanu Valley. Then they moved out to the Manoa Valley, Waikiki, Kahala, Alewa Heights, Pacific Heights, and Makiki Heights. Even that changed as circumstances brought other nationalities into the areas, and after World War II the new development for the well-to-do was on the Wailupe Peninsula, on Portlock Road, and in Kailua. There was one exception. At the end of World War II, a building boom developed, and one of the areas that opened up was the very attractive slope of Tantalus, where the air was cool and clear. The tract was put up for competitive bidding, and the people with the most ready cash were the winners. They happened to be old Chinese families with long backgrounds and large reserves. As the area became built up with fine homes, people gave it the name Mandarin Heights. As time went on, the families changed; others got more money; and the old Chinese died off. Mandarin Heights in the 1970's could not be said to be controlled by anything other than money.

As the Americans took over the Hawaiian Islands, first as missionaries, then as traders, then as planters, then as revolutionaries, their one great fear was that the Japanese might turn the islands into a Japanese colony. At the time of annexation the Japanese racial strain predominated in the islands, and by the 1920's the Occidentals feared that the Japanese might take control and that the words spoken by the governor in 1907 might come true: "Hawaii presents the anomaly never dreamed of by any founders of our Republic, of a land under the American flag in which the dominant sentiment is loyaty to a foreign emperor."

By 1930, an educational commission warned, Hawaii might see an electorate that was 28 percent Japanese, and by 1940 the Japanese might have 47 percent of the votes. This kind of talk created some consternation in Washington, D.C., and set back the cause of statehood a number of years.

To combat such talk, educators and missionaries set about creating patriotism in Hawaii with new zeal. The Reverend Takie Okumura began a program with the older residents, the Issei who had immigrated long ago. In 1927 he began a series of conferences for "new Americans" of Japanese ancestry. Leaders of business, industry, and the professions were persuaded to come to these conferences and talk with the young Japanese, telling them of the opportunities in America and also committing themselves to the extension of those opportunities. These conferences continued right up to the summer of 1941, when there was much talk of war between Japan and the United States. The subject of the last meeting of these young people was "Our Present Patriotic Responsibilities."

Hawaiians of all shades of color had in fact long shown a very high degree of American patriotism. In World War I the Hawaiian War Relief Committee, which became the local Red Cross chapter, raised hundreds of thousands of dollars for relief effort. In addition, Hawaiians of all varieties made quantities of surgical dressings and other supplies for shipment to the war areas. In the matter of the Liberty Loans—the war bonds—only one state in the Union surpassed the record of Hawaii.

The strength of this feeling of belonging was shown in the

next few years. In 1923 Hawaii's Governor Farrington led in the creation of Hawaii's bill of rights, which was an effort to promote statehood by asserting the rights of the Hawaiians to the treatment given other Americans. From this came the extension of federal highway, education, agricultural, and other programs, which had earlier been available only to the citizens of the forty-eight states.

When the Japanese attacked Pearl Harbor, the thought flashed through many minds in Hawaii as well as on the mainland that the Japanese nationalists and the Japanese immigrants to Hawaii would be a danger. Immediately, the FBI picked up the Japanese consular staff in Honolulu and the two hundred other consular agents scattered throughout the islands. Altogether, though, only fourteen hundred Hawaiian residents were actually held on suspicion, and when they were sorted out, only 1 percent of the Japanese population of the islands was regarded as a bad risk and sent to the mainland camps.

There were no more loyal Americans than the Hawaiians. When the bombs were falling on Pearl Harbor, civilian doctors and nurses, many of them Japanese, rushed to the hospitals to help the wounded. Of the first thirty-six civilians killed in this attack twenty were people of Japanese ancestry living in the residential district of Honolulu.

One bad incident occurred. On the tiny island of Niihau, not one of the 150 inhabitants knew of the Pearl Harbor raid because they had no radios. One of the Japanese airmen attacking Pearl Harbor was forced down there. Howard Kaleohano, a Hawaiian of Polynesian descent, saw bullet holes in the plane and suspected that something was wrong, so he took away the Japanese pilot's gun, papers, and maps and buried them.

Because of the excitement of the war, the weekly launch from Kauai did not arrive. In the meantime, the Japanese pilot sought out the two Japanese residents of Niihau, one an alien, the other an American citizen. They helped the aviator escape from his guard and then dismantled the two machine guns from the Japanese plane. The three Japanese then began a reign of terror on Niihau.

All night that first night the Japanese terrorized the people. Kaleohano and five others escaped to the beach, found a boat, and began to row toward Kauai. In their absence the Japanese burned down Kaleohano's house. The next morning they cornered another Hawaiian, Benjamin Kanahele, and forced him to make a search for Kaleohano and the papers and maps. When he did not produce the incriminating documents, the Japanese pilot shot him three times, in the hip, thigh, and chest.

Kanahele got angry. He picked up the Japanese pilot and bashed his brains out against a wall. His wife grabbed the one Japanese-American, who committed suicide with his own gun. The other Japanese was taken into custody soon enough, for Kaleohano and his companions rowed for sixteen hours, made port in Kauai, and brought the authorities.

Such was the outcry of the Japanese in Hawaii against this disloyalty that the incident did not provoke any racial demonstrations or a panic about Japanese loyalty.

The military records of the territory told a great deal of the truth about the Hawaiian Orientals and the war. Thousands of Hawaiians went into the service. More than half of them were Japanese; 15 percent were Occidentals; 10 percent were Chinese; 12 percent were Hawaiian or part Hawaiian; and 9 percent were Filipino. Japanese, Chinese, Filipino, and every other variety of Hawaiian opened their homes to servicemen. They organized the United Service Organizations and the special services shows for the camps. The Boy Scouts, the Girl Scouts, and all the other organizations dedicated themselves to the war effort.

It was not long before the authorities began to realize that the martial law declared for Hawaii on Pearl Harbor day was not going to be necessary. Early in 1943 civil government was largely restored to the territory. All through the Pacific conflict there was not a single incident of sabotage or any indication of disloyalty by any Hawaiian, other than the Niihau incident of the first moments of the war. Nor was there the slightest evidence in all this time of any "bloc voting" or concerted activity on the part of Japanese Hawaiians. Japanese candidates for public office all withdrew during the war, so that they would not embarrass their fellow Hawaiians with the people back on the mainland. In 1943, for the first time in nearly half a century, not a single Japanese sat in the Hawaiian legislature.

It was not easy for the Japanese at first. When the war broke out, one of Gen. Walter Short's first acts was to suspend the Hawaiian Territorial Guard, because it had so many Japanese members. Of these men 160 volunteered to do any work at all to show their loyalty, and when Gen. Delos Emmons replaced Short, he attached these young men to a regiment of engineers. They spent months working at all kinds of jobs, including simple digging, although many of them were highly skilled and most of them were college students. Finally, they were allowed to enlist in the service.

The two national guard regiments were later put together and 1,300 Japanese-Americans were assigned to the 100th Infantry Battalion, which served at Anzio and in a number of other battles. Within ten months 300 men had been killed in action and 650 were wounded. Army men called it "The Purple Heart Battalion." Finally, it was so weakened that it had to be absorbed into the 442nd Battalion, another Nisei battalion.

In Hawaii virtually all Japanese who were eligible and able volunteered for war work or for military service, and when the WACs were organized in Hawaii, most of the volunteers were Japanese.

Hawaii came out of the war with its honor intact, and more than that, with a strong feeling by all concerned that whether one was Japanese or Chinese or haole or Hawaiian or Portuguese or anything else did not make any difference at all.

That is not to say that life has always been easy for Orientals in Hawaii. Quite the contrary. In the beginning the haoles exploited all the other races shamefully. So did the Oriental traders who came early in the game. There was an old saying that in Hawaii there were three pay scales on a descending basis: what haoles paid haoles, what haoles paid Hawaiians and Orientals, and what Orientals paid Orientals.

Unionism came to Hawaii in the 1880's, but it was the whites-only unionism of the American Federation of Labor. The Japanese organized their own federation of labor in 1919, as did the Filipinos, to try to secure better treatment. In 1919 these groups began a strike which lasted seven months and ended in violence on both sides. Filipinos and some Chinese became strikebreakers, and this difficulty led to some of the little racial tension that ever cursed Hawaii.

By the middle of the 1920's, however, the Oriental unionists were banding together, and in the 1930's they were taken under the wing of the Congress of Industrial Organizations, particularly the longshore and maritime unions. By the end of the Pacific war, unionism was strong in Hawaii. In the 1950's, when the objectors to Hawaiian statehood came along, as they always did, they were no longer worried about race so much as about the specter of communism that seemed to frighten all America. Even that passed eventually.

As far as business was concerned, the haoles at first completely dominated the field, but the Chinese and Japanese traders did well too. The Big Five, American and British companies organized by Occidentals, continued to overshadow Hawaiian life for many years. Only in the war and postwar years did the Orientals seize upon an old Hawaiian custom of forming hui, which are informal syndicates. Through them the smaller businessmen can raise capital quickly and compete with the big businesses.

The Big Five still dominate Hawaii, but the smaller businessmen, particularly the Orientals, are producing their own share of millionaires in the 1970's. The years since the end of World War II and statehood have produced a great leveling of the incomes and the social attitudes of all groups and all races in Hawaii.

Chapter Eleven

The New Society

One of the most heartening bits of evidence of the resiliency of the American system is the history of race relations in the United States since the end of World War II. One could not expect many minority groups to agree with that statement *now,* but from a retrospective view a few years hence, they too will see how much has been accomplished in so short a time.

That is not to say that racism is dead in America, any more than it is dead in Africa, China, Japan, or any other country. There will always be people in all lands who stretch the limits of national and racial pride to assume a superiority that really does not exist. The acid test is in the behavior of governments. Almost everywhere, except in the Republic of South Africa, Rhodesia, and a few black African states, the policy of racism is dead. There are hangovers, such as in Southern and border American states and in big cities and rich suburbs that resist racial integration, but these are local matters and the pressures of society are changing the mores.

As far as Orientals in America are concerned, the change has been almost complete in the past thirty years. Even at the outbreak of the Pacific war, Chinese, Japanese, Korean, Filipino, and other Oriental Americans were not regarded as "real Americans" by a majority of people. Their rights, if not actually limited, were always in danger. They were "different," and so they were not treated the same as other Americans. Indeed, until World War II there was a strong popular, if uninformed, belief that Orientals were physically different from Occidentals, that their eyes and other organs were constructed in a different manner. It was nonsense, but a nonsense that was accepted in many quarters.

The Pacific war completely changed the lives of the American Chinese, for example. When the Chinese-American soldiers and sailors returned from the war in 1945, they found that the old restrictive covenants on real estate had become illegal. They could live anywhere they wanted to, and the federal government, through G.I. and F.H.A. loans, helped them do it.

Then more Chinese began going to college, and more of them found it possible, even easy, to get good jobs. The civil service did not discriminate. The state governments did not discriminate. More, there were new jobs with big corporations and small companies. These young business and professional people began moving to the suburbs, to the shore of Marin County north of San Francisco, to the peninsula outside San Francisco.

Early in the 1960's Chinatown, San Francisco, was very much in danger of a decline that would have made it a blighted area of the city, when it was already becoming known far and wide as a tourist attraction for the area. President Johnson's abolition of all laws limiting immigration on the basis of nationality opened the doors to a new Chinese migration. Under the law the quota for Chinese was twenty thousand persons per year. This meant free immigration leading to naturalization.

Because of the civil war in China, many of the new immigrants were professional and technical people. Many of them have found good jobs in universities and hospitals and businesses, and have moved into suburban homes in good districts.

Whole families of working-class people have also come to America from China by way of Hong Kong, and their story is not so positive. They have been the new immigrants to Chinatown. They came speaking little or none of the language, and that immediately created an employment problem. Then in the 1960's and 1970's the worsening American economy cut down the number of jobs available. Whether or not it was caused by residual prejudice by some labor unions and some hiring halls, the Chinese often remained unemployed. Learning English can usually get them out of trouble, but some simply are not equipped to learn a new language. They suffer.

The real test of the old American melting-pot theory comes right down to something that has always made racists shudder. Some call it miscegenation. The civilized word for it is intermarriage.

Special problems have been faced by the Asian women who came to America as war brides. Sometimes these marriages have been very unhappy. In fact, the divorce rate for mixed marriages at Fort Lewis, the big military base near Seattle, was running to 80 percent in 1974. Thus only about 20 percent of the marriages contracted overseas between Caucasian Americans and Japanese, Korean, Vietnamese, and Thai girls were successful after a year or two. The basic problems are the language and cultural differences, as in the case of Park Song Yu, a pretty Korean girl who married an American serviceman stationed at Inchon.

Park Song Yu grew up in a typical Korean family, living in a Korean house heated against the biting winds of wintertime by charcoal braziers. She wore rubber shoes and long dresses, and she went to school for eight years. Then she got a job in a restaurant as a waitress, and there she met her future husband, an American army technician. They courted for several months. His knowledge of the Korean language was rudimentary, and so was her English, but love conquered that cultural difficulty. What James, her future husband, liked about Park Song Yu was her manners. She had grown up in a society where it was the woman's role to please her husband, and the whole family revolved around his wishes. So her whole approach to James was to please him. Never had he known an American girl who was so amenable.

They were married just before James's enlistment ran out, and they came back to America when he reenlisted. They were assigned to Fort Lewis, where many of the men who have Asian wives have been assigned. At first it seemed very easy for Park Song Yu. She met a number of Korean girls, who were also married to Americans. There were Japanese and Vietnamese, too, but Park Song Yu found she had virtually nothing in common with these girls—perhaps even less than with the Caucasian wives of servicemen.

Park Song Yu decided she wanted to be more like an American wife, and she wanted to get a job. James did not mind, for he was busy all day at the fort. She began looking for work, but her poor English kept her from getting a job as a waitress or in a shop. She did find a job in a massage parlor; one of the skills she had learned in Korea was that of massage. But this job came to an end when the Seattle *Times* and other newspapers began publishing articles about prostitution in the sauna and massage places, and James forced her to quit.

Little rifts began to develop in their marriage. She could tell that James was sometimes impatient when he spoke quickly in English and she failed to grasp his meaning. Back in Inchon he had claimed a real liking for Korean food, but now he developed a distaste for kimchi, the basic Korean spiced pickle, and other Korean dishes. Once when she had prepared a festive dinner, he came home and said he had already eaten at the club, and he refused to taste it.

Park Song Yu saw Japanese and other girls who had thrown off the old ways and were becoming independent like American girls. She began to dislike the way James ordered her around and expected her to wait on him. So they quarreled, and one quarrel led to another. Finally, James suggested that they get a divorce, and Park Song Yu felt it was the only way for them.

She then had the big problem of deciding whether to stay on in America or to go home to Korea. She decided to stay, for although America was strange, she had already broken her ties with Korea. So she found another Korean ex-wife who was in the same situation, and they took a little apartment together. Both got jobs in sauna parlors. Life was not very happy, but Park Song Yu was able to live.

Another kind of Asian problem is that presented by the unwanted children fathered by American servicemen in Asian lands. Another Park—a boy named Park Yung Do—was one of these children of a mixed union. He was born in a village two hundred miles from Seoul, after his mother had an affair with an American serviceman. The mother's parents refused to accept the little boy of mixed heritage, and before he was eleven years old, he was thrown out into the street. He kept alive only because he was bright enough to attach himself to a bar where American servicemen gathered. He ran errands for the soldiers and earned a little money in tips from them. That was all he had.

One day a soldier told him about the Holt Adoption Agency in Seoul. If he could get there, a couple in America might adopt him. So Park saved his money and bought a bus ticket to Seoul. One day he showed up on the doorstep of the Holt agency. They took him in, and he stayed on until he was adopted by Mr. and Mrs. Harold Tinney of Buckley, Washington. They paid Park's passage to America, and early in 1974 he came to live with them and their three other children.

Park's name was changed officially to Michael Tinney. At first he had trouble with the language, but when one is thirteen years old, a new language is not a problem that lasts long. He entered public school with his new brothers and sisters and was very soon acclimated to America.

Newly arrived Asians in the West face many, many problems. In 1974 there were an estimated two million Asians in the United States, concentrated in the Western states for the most part. They are beset by five basic difficulties: cultural barriers, family problems, educational problems, poverty, and lack of resources. There is very little information about some of these Asians because in modern times they have not concentrated in the ghettos as in the past, but are scattered among the population.

In various Pacific states some strides are now being made to meet their problems. Universities and communities have begun holding workshops and discussions of the problems that beset Asians just trying to settle into American life. In Tacoma, Washington, a community college sponsored an Asian-American retreat in February, 1974, that set the stage for study of some of the real problems. So progress is being made.

After World War II another kind of newcomer came to the United States. Mrs. M. J. Fung came from a very wealthy Chinese family. Her grandfather was a tutor to the Ch'ing emperor, the last of the dynasty, and the emperor gave him many fine art treasures. Some of those treasures found their way to the Fung house in San Francisco.

When Mrs. Fung was a girl, her family had several homes, in Shanghai and other cities and the country. The country homes had gardens as large as small city parks, and visitors came to see the beautiful estates and the flowers. The family also owned the village where the main country house was located. All this, of course, was before the Chino-Japanese War, which changed life tremendously.

This young girl grew up in a typical well-to-do Chinese family. The grandparents owned the house, and Grandmother was the *tai-tai,* or mistress of all she surveyed. There were no quarrels—such were not considered proper. Each child had a nursemaid. The family had so many servants that no one turned a hand at any sort of housework. When Grandfather had a birthday, the celebration lasted an entire week, with feasts of duck, fish, geese, chicken, pork, and rare vegetables and fruits, and with snacks and meals served at any hour of the day.

Such was the life of the rich Chinese—a round of entertainment with plenty of time for contemplation—but all that changed after the 1940's, when the Fungs came to San Francisco and opened a silk and art goods store on Grant Avenue. However, in either world, Chinese or American, the Fungs were recognized as being of the privileged class.

Not so most Chinese. Unemployment in San Francisco's Chinatown was estimated at 13 percent in 1971. Heavy immigration and its attendant problems led to a new exploitation of these workers, and a new demand by labor people that the immigration be stopped. For a while the same old 1870's story seemed to be playing one more time in the American theater, but this time government and labor, working together, took steps to better the lot of the Chinese workers, rather than drive them away.

The new Chinatown has had new problems. One of them

has been the emergence of street gangs, stemming from the poverty of the people, but here the attitude is a new one. The young Chinese are not subservient, not afraid. They may be resentful, but it is not so much because of race as because of economic problems.

One of the most important factors in this flattening out of the race problem has been the emergence of the People's Republic of China as a major world power. Long before the United States government began direct dealings with Mao Tse-tung and Chou En-lai, most Americans had begun to respect the new China, if not to love it, and that respect has brought with it a feeling of pride on the part of many of the Chinese-American youth. It was not so much a question of politics—although politics certainly has its part in Chinese-American thinking—as it was a question of belonging.

Just before the collapse of the Nationalist regime in China, there had been an effort by many people of goodwill in China to seek a middle road, which was represented by the Democratic League of China. But if one asked many Chinese in those days what they thought of the Democratic League, one was likely to get a cynical answer. "It is a fine idea, but the League does not have an army."

That same attitude colors the thinking of young Chinese-Americans today. They are proud of the People's Republic because it amounts to something. Henry Kissinger and President Nixon went to Peking; Mao and Chou did not come to Washington. And that was meaningful; it gave young Chinese-Americans a feeling that they were "someone."

Chinese restaurants can be found in almost any American community of any size. The Chinese have also made many cultural and social contributions to the Western world. Going back a very long way, they brought silks and spices. Marco Polo went to China in the thirteenth century and returned to the Italian states with the Chinese noodle, which became the basis for spaghetti. The Chinese invented gunpowder and paper and a system of astronomy. All these gifts came to the West, but in a manner so diffuse that most people do not even recognize them as Chinese.

In more modern times Chinese-Americans and Chinese in America have made other contributions. The most recent and most celebrated, of course, is acupuncture, an old form of Chinese medicine that has caught on in America. James Reston, the New York *Times* columnist, went to China just after the thaw in relations, contracted acute appendicitis, and had an operation in which the anesthesia used was acupuncture. He wrote about it, and the resulting publicity brought changes to the whole medical world. The Chinese, without fanfare, have been practicing acupuncture in China for a thousand years; now they also practice it in Washington and other American cities.

The end of the Pacific war sent home thousands of Americans who had been exposed to China and who had developed a taste for Chinese food beyond the old chop suey and chow mein. Thus, in the big cities like San Francisco, Los Angeles, Chicago, Washington, and New York, the Chinese have brought in a new style in restaurants. Americans in China discovered that Chinese food was not "cheap," as it usually had been in America. Some of the new Chinese-American restaurants vie with the best in the world in any cuisine, for Chinese cuisine is, in fact, one of the leading methods of cooking in the world. Some gourmets say that there are only two basic cuisines of any importance—the French school, based on butter cookery, and the Chinese school, based on the soybean. Hungarians and Vietnamese and Japanese would deny this, of course, but throughout the ages these two basic styles have certainly developed.

Only in recent years have Chinese cookbooks become common in most American kitchens. In China there were virtually no cookbooks, for dishes were handed down from family to family and region to region by word of mouth. In the past decade, however, scores of Chinese cookbooks have been published in America. They have led finally to a cookbook prepared by Craig Claiborne and a Chinese associate, and a Chinese encyclopedia of cooking that in some ways rivals the Larousse gastronomic encyclopedia.

Chinese styles such as the *cheongsam,* or slit dress, and Chinese robes have in recent years influenced Western fashions. Chinese art has come into American salons. Dong Kingman, a Chinese-American watercolorist, is one of the most famous of American artists. Chinese literature in translation is becoming more widely read in the United States, and some Chinese and Chinese-American authors have achieved considerable fame. Lau Shaw, the auther of *Ricksha Boy* is one; Lin Yutang, the professor, gourmet, and novelist, is another. His writings on China have touched the heart of all the world.

Chinese physicists were instrumental in much of the serious work on atomic management at the University of California. Several of them have since returned to Peking to put their experience to work. American architecture owes many serious debts to I. M. Pei, the industrious and sometimes revolutionary Chinese architect. In a hundred other fields one can find Chinese contributions to the mainstream of American life, or to that of the whole Western culture for that matter.

Frank Chin, the Chinese-American author, has denied that this means much in terms of the assimilation of the Chinese. Many young Chinese-Americans have the same feeling. It is their belief that the true integrity and dignity of Chinese-Americans will come about only when they manage to come to terms with their own racial ethnic tradition, as it fits into the American society. In 1969 some of these people founded the Combined Asian Research Project to develop the Chinese heritage in America.

As for politics, which might be seen as a very real common

denominator of public thinking, Asians have in recent years begun to emerge as effective parts of the community. Back in 1954 a Sikh named Dalip Saund Singh from Riverside, California, won his district's congressional election and went to Congress. He served ably for several years. Dalip Saund Singh had come to this country as an immigrant and had, through his own efforts, brought himself into the total society in which he lived.

Other Asians were slower perhaps, but not entirely because of their own inclinations. Until the 1950's and 1960's the conditions were not quite ripe on the mainland of the United States. But in 1972 Dr. Chin Lee, a Washington physician, ran for the office of nonvoting delegate to Congress from the District of Columbia. He was defeated by the Reverend Walter Fauntroy, a black man. In 1973 in Seattle, Liem Tuai, another Chinese-American, ran for mayor of the city. He already held the post of president of the City Council and was a successful practicing attorney—all signs of a basic change in the American scene. His father had been a cook who immigrated to this country.

For a look at even more intense Oriental participation in American politics, one need turn only to Hawaii. One of the United States senators is a Chinese-American—Hiram Fong. The other is a Japanese-American—Daniel Inouye. Both Congressmen Spark Matsunaga of Honolulu and Patsy Takemoto Mink of Waipahu are Japanese-Americans. The roster of major state officials of Hawaii reads like an international directory. Governor John A. Burns is a haole. Lt. Governor George R. Ariyoshi and Superintendent of Public Instruction Shiro Amioka are Japanese-Americans. Treasurer Hiram R. Kamaka's name represents Hawaiian heritage. Attorney General George Pai's last name is Chinese, and Auditor KeNam Kim's name is Korean.

Hawaii is obviously leading the nation in bringing about changes in the matter of race, and this is true in every way. One tends to think of Orientals in the Western world as being generally poor, with a few very rich mandarins among them, but in Hawaii the median annual income of Chinese by 1960 was $1,500 *higher* than that of any other group, including the Occidentals in the islands. The Japanese were lower, but not by very much.

When the peoples of this nation cease to think of themselves as Chinese, Occidental, Hawaiian, Latvian, Japanese, or Russian, that is true assimilation. Hawaii is America's testing ground for Oriental-Occidental assimilation, just as New York has been the testing ground for Jewish-Gentile assimilation or Boston for Irish Catholic–Puritan Protestant assimilation. Three generations ago any American political analyst could assure his readers that a Roman Catholic could never be president of the United States. Not ever. Well, none was for a long time. Al Smith, one of the most gifted politicians in America, was defeated for the presidency in 1928, almost entirely because he was a Roman Catholic. But in 1960 John F. Kennedy, a Roman Catholic, was elected. It became obvious then that anything could happen in America if the people willed it so.

In Hawaii twentieth-century Americans are watching a new phenomenon. It is the rapid disappearance of any racial sense among the people who have elected to be Hawaiians and Americans. In 1912 only 12 percent of the marriages were interracial. By 1932 the rate had risen to 32 percent. By 1945 it had risen to 38.5 percent. So much had the islands changed that those trying to study race had to deal with sixty-four different possible racial combinations, and the business of trying to keep racial statistics was becoming meaningless. In the 1960's and 1970's, it became even more meaningless, as young people found virtually no differences between themselves, or at least they found so many similarities in backgrounds and ideas that the differences became merely spice for life.

That is not to say that the process of biological fusion is going to be immediate. Some people who are blond and blue-eyed prefer other people who are blond and blue-eyed, and that will have a part in the mixture for a long time to come. But that is a far cry from the old racist attitudes. As sociologist Andrew Lind of the University of Hawaii put it, "The peoples of Hawaii are becoming Hawaii's people."

Perhaps some of the difference between Hawaii and the American mainland can be accounted for by the gentleness of the original Polynesian owners of Hawaii in the matter of race. Perhaps some can be attributed to such influences as Takie Okumura's schools. Among other things he established 163 Japanese-language schools in the islands. These schools not only taught the language to the youngsters, but also taught them about the society in which they lived.

On the mainland changes have also been great, however. Chinatown, U.S.A., has lost its point of focus as the center of Chinese-American life and will lose it more as Chinese-Americans and other Americans find they can buy *tofu, bok choy,* fresh ginger, and other Chinese foods in the local supermarkets. This is already true in many areas, both because of the outspread of Chinese-Americans to the suburbs and because of the internationalization of American eating habits, brought about by the constant succession of wars in the Orient in which America has been involved since 1941.

Chinese- and Japanese-Americans would not agree that racism has ended in the continental United States or that theirs is the best of all possible worlds. Many, both young and old, complain that living standards, opportunities in the business world, and general way of life are still not the same for them as for their Occidental counterparts. Yet the high intermarriage rate of Japanese-Americans with Occidentals in the 1970's is an interesting development. In the year 1971, in Fresno County, California, once the scene of bloody anti-Japanese violence, 49 percent of the Japanese married outside the Japanese community, as compared with only 18 percent in 1958. This statistic indicates that what is happening on the mainland is not so different, after all, from what is happening in Hawaii.

In all these matters, a significant factor in change has been the intermingling of cultures. In the old days the only contact between the cultures was missionary work, with such fillips as the founding of the Peking Union Medical College by the Rockefeller Foundation. In the postwar world the cultural exchange has a much broader basis. Students from all over the world and many from the Asian world flocked to the United States at the end of World War II to study. This exchange and the sending of Americans abroad was facilitated largely by the Fulbright program of grants and scholarships, designed by the senator from Arkansas, who had been a Rhodes scholar and university president himself. So Americans began studying Japanese and Chinese to the point where these studies are no longer regarded as an exotic phenomenon in academic life. As those Americans learned, they began to appreciate and to pass that appreciation on to other Americans. One example might be the establishment by Charles Tuttle of Rutland, Vermont, of a book-publishing enterprise in Tokyo.

Tuttle went to Japan as a result of World War II and married a girl belonging to a well-to-do Japanese family. He came from a Vermont family of booksellers and publishers, and nothing was more natural than for him to engage in his speciality. He began publishing in English various books by Japanese and other Asians, but he did it by remaining in Japan for the most part, and bringing to the West the fine literature, art, and culture of the Far East. His books of Japanese, Chinese, and other Asian art have won many prizes. He "discovered" for the West beauties that had not been seen before.

Concurrently a new appreciation of Japanese literature

developed in the United States' literary community. For half a century most of the American interpretation of China had come from Pearl Buck's novels, but there had been no Pearl Buck for Japan. After World War II Japanese novelists caught on in America, just as Indian novelists did. Housewives flocked to the library to get the latest copy of Santha Rama-Rau's work or one of the new Japanese novels.

Chinese-American critics are right when they say that no Chinese-American "great" had appeared on the American scene by 1970. This was less true of the Japanese, perhaps because of their wartime struggle. Toru Matsumoto, a Nisei, wrote the first book about the Nisei in America, to explain to his fellow Americans the feelings of this minority. Bill Hosokawa wrote the most recent and authoritative book on this subject, *Nisei: The Quiet Americans,* which was published in 1969. *No-No Boy* by John Okada was a novel based on the trials of the Japanese-Americans.

Japanese-Americans are also active in other fields of expression in the 1970's. Miné Okubo is a Japanese painter. Isamu Noguchi is a well-known Japanese-American sculptor, who blends the ideas of Eastern and Western art. Japanese and Chinese techniques of painting have intrigued many Occidental American artists in the twentieth century, and it is not at all unusual to attend a local outdoor art show, find paintings in the Oriental style, and then discover that the artist is blond and blue-eyed, and never traveled west of St. Louis.

All schoolchildren in the land know that origami is a system of Japanese paper folding that makes delightful toys. Americans have learned to write Japanese poetry, and one Occidental, Lucille Nixon of Palo Alto, won honorable mention in the emperor's contest in Tokyo one year. That certainly shows a new mixture of American culture.

The Oriental art museum of the University of Oregon, the Freer gallery in Washington, and the collection of the

Metropolitan Museum of Art have long been famous in America. Much newer are such matters as the publication by the Philadelphia Museum of Art of Tseng Yu-ho Ecke's *Chinese Calligraphy,* a study of Chinese writing that is also an art form in Asia.

Sumo wrestlers have been brought to America in recent years to stage bouts. In addition, Chinese street gang youths have taken considerable pride in their practice of the militaristic offensive technique called *kung fu.* Nearly every American youth understands *kung fu* in the 1970's, because of a television series based on a Chinese character. The Japanese have been teaching judo and aikido, forms of defense, exercise, and self-discipline, for many years. A Korean entrepreneur in Washington has made a fortune teaching the Korean variation of these manly arts. "Nobody bothers me," squeaks a tiny tot who has just upset a potential attacker in the television commercial.

These particular arts may be a manifestation of something not quite nice in American society, but there has been much, much more.

Oriental religions, too, have assumed a new importance in the Western world. The presence of a guru, or Indian religious leader, no longer brings the stares of the curious in any large American community. Americans have taken up the study of yoga very seriously, and classes in yoga have been offered on television just as casually as those in physical fitness. Zen Buddhism captured a whole American school generation in the 1960's. Shintoism, Confucianism, and Taoism have gained new adherents in the West. What is more important, this new understanding on the part of many Westerners indicates their tolerance for standards of existence that are different from their own.

S. I. Hayakawa, the late Japanese educator, who became president of San Francisco State College and saw that embattled institution through its difficult days of radicalization, also became a household figure in America through a popular newspaper column. Readers and others quickly learned that Hayakawa was, to be sure, a Japanese-American, but that, first of all, he was an American.

With so many Asians going into their third and fourth generation in America, we find that much has changed and much is changing. The future looks even brighter than it did for the Nisei who came back with their shields from the wars. New words have come into the Japanese-American vocabulary—"Sansei," meaning the children of Nisei, and "Yonsei," meaning the Sansei's children. The Sansei are taller than their fathers, who were taller than their fathers, largely because of diet. The Yonsei are so thoroughly Americanized in speech and habit that no one could possibly tell their racial origin over the telephone, an acid test of "difference."

Some Nisei, Chinese-Americans, and others have come to the conclusion that to resolve its social differences America must abandon the old melting-pot theory, which called for the homogenization of the society. The optimists among these thinkers look forward to a society in which differences are accepted and even cultivated, where the Japanese-Americans keep largely to themselves, as do the Chinese-Americans, but mingle freely in public places and have all the true requisites and perquisites of citizenship. Bill Hosokawa, in ending his book on the Nisei, expressed the hope and belief that this was the direction in which America was heading.

But Hawaii and Fresno County and other areas point to something quite different—the actual realization of the melting pot after a period of time. The big American race problem in the postwar years has *not* been the assimilation or accommodation of the Orientals. Perhaps that is one reason their progress has been so rapid and the results so visible. Were a hundred thousand American blacks suddenly to be shipped to Honolulu and dumped on the Hawaiian shore, much in the manner in which population moves occurred in the nineteenth century, it might well be that there would be a racial uprising in Hawaii too—for racism, as has been shown so many times in so many places, is almost totally an economic matter. For the Orientals in America, the great improvement has come with their ability to compete, and such an offer of opportunity is still the most visibly workable solution to racial problems.

Chapter Twelve

Life in America

Anyone who reads this book, or any other book for that matter, is indebted to the Chinese, for they invented paper and the movable type that made it useful. Over a thousand years ago, while the Western world was still living in the Dark Ages, the Chinese were printing books and pictures.

Many of these gifts came to the Western world by way of the overland route to Europe. Marco Polo and many others traveled that way. Some gifts came to the West by way of the Arab world and Africa, for the Chinese traded with these people as early as the time of Christ. Only in recent times did the gifts come directly across the Pacific, with the immigration of the nineteenth century described in this book.

Why would a young Chinese who did not speak English come to America as a worker in the 1850's or the 1860's, stay ten or twenty years, go home, and then return to America? The reason is simple enough—money. While in America, such Chinese migrants made no real attempt to adopt the ways of the Westerners. Why not? The reason again is simple: Until the past two generations of Chinese, the men and few women who came here were not thinking of themselves as Americans, but as Chinese.

If one understands a basic fact of Chinese culture, all this becomes clear: In China, until the present revolution, the family was everything, the individual nothing. Thus a Cantonese peasant family would without a qualm send a young man like Chin Fong Chow from his village outside Canton to make his way in America.

Chin came in 1868. He was no ordinary Chinese, but became president of the Yan-wo Company, one of the big trading houses and importers of Chinese labor. Yet in spite of his silks and jades, Chin Fong Chow was as much a servant of his family as the lowliest coolie. He accepted voluntary exile to the far land of America to serve the interests of that family, and whether or not he would ever return home would depend on the family council. While he was in America, he was the faithful servant of the family. He lived in Chinese style in San Francisco's Chinatown in an unpretentious house decorated luxuriously inside. He kept a little shrine where he and his wife and children paid obeisance to their ancestors. He attended the Chinese temple, where he worshiped the old gods. At home he dressed in Chinese costume, although he might adopt Occidental suits for the street. He ate Chinese food cooked in the Chinese fashion by a Chinese cook and used Chinese dishes. His whole life was wrapped up in Chinatown and in China itself. Even if he might never dream of returning to China, if that was the family's will, his heart would always be there, and he would arrange to have his family bring his body or the ashes back to China when he died, to be buried in the family burying place, so he would join his ancestors.

All his life long Chin Fong Chow believed in the essential

superiority of Chinese culture to that of the Western world. Those miners who wanted to cut off pigtails and the street boys of San Francisco who harried the Chinese were no better than savages to him, for he knew full well how much Chinese civilization had to offer.

One story perhaps illustrates, as well as anything, how different the old Chinese way of looking at life was from that of the Western world. Back in the days of the Han dynasty, China was beset by the ferocious Huns from the Western steppes of Asia. The emperor sent an ambassador named Chang Ch'ien across the wasteland of Turkestan to find and make an alliance with one certain friendly tribe in the west. This alliance was supposed to help the Han emperor defeat the savage warriors.

Soon after leaving China on his mission, Chang Ch'ien was captured by the very Huns he was trying to help defeat. He was held prisoner by them *for ten years*. At the end of that time he escaped. And then what did he do? An American would imagine that he would have returned to China, told of his adventures, and sought a new life. Not so. Chang Ch'ien headed westward once more, went to the extreme west of Turkestan, found the tribe in question, and discussed the alliance. On his way home he was again captured by the Huns. After a year he escaped and returned to the Chinese capital to report on his mission. No one thought there was anything odd or abnormal about his behavior.

Is it any wonder then that Chin Fong Chow or the other Chinese who came to America in the nineteenth century had a different kind of time sense than the Americans they encountered? The Chinese way depended not only on time, but on a sense of subjugation of personality, which still exists in China, and which makes the Oriental seem strange to Westerners. "Ego" and "self-expression" are Westerners' words. Such concepts are quite foreign to the East.

The Chinese and the Japanese gave the Western world

silk. The Chinese also gave us tea, which the British made famous by going all around the world in their trading ships. The Chinese also gave us porcelain, and that is why we call it china. It is quite different from the ordinary pottery that was known to other societies. It is made from a clay containing aluminum silica, which was first found in the hills of central China. When this clay was mixed with a mineral called petuntse and baked, it became porcelain. The Chinese were making fine porcelain objects in the year A.D. 300. It took fourteen hundred years for the Western world to learn how to do it.

Chin Fong Chow, in his Chinese house in San Francisco, ate from his porcelain plates and contemplated the superiority of his culture. In the evenings, as the breeze blew in across the Golden Gate, he would pick up a bound bundle of rice paper and begin to read—perhaps commentaries on the life and works of Confucius or the life of that other great Chinese philosopher and religious leader, Lao-tze.

Back in the fifth century before Christ, a philosopher named Mo Ti did much the same thing as Chin Fong Chow. Mo Ti carried three cartloads of bamboo books whenever he had to travel. Around A.D. 105 Ts'ai Lun put together a substance made of tree bark, hemp, rags, and fish nets, which became paper. Seven hundred years later the Chinese were printing beautiful books on paper. A hundred years after that they printed nine of the major Chinese classics of literature in 130 volunes.

Was it any wonder then that Chin Fong Chow could not be impressed with the Western society around him, which seemed so inferior in every way to his own?

On the Chinese New Year, which is based on the Chinese calendar, Chin Fong Chow and his family set off firecrackers, arranged a feast or two, and celebrated the coming of another season. Firecrackers date back to the seventh century A.D. and the Chinese invention of gunpowder. They used gunpowder in 1232 to frighten the Mongols in the siege of Kaifeng. How the lip of Chin Fong Chow must have curled as he observed the killings and violence of the Westerners, who had turned gunpowder from a thing of beauty into a thing of death in California. The Chinese, with all their knowledge, had never chosen to use gunpowder to blow up their world.

At his dinner table at night, Chin Fong Chow liked a little fruit after finishing the rice and duck and pork dishes. One of his favorites was an orange, introduced in Europe by the Arabs, and still called the "Chinese apple" in Holland. When the Westerners were burning villages and pillaging one another more than a thousand years ago, the Chinese were cultivating oranges, lemons, and the pomelo, which is the ancestor of the grapefruit.

Once Chin Fong Chow was replete with food he would go out into his garden in the quiet of the San Francisco evening and look at his roses and chrysanthemums, both brought to the West from China. There, with the azaleas, camellias, asters, and tree peonies, he would be happy for an hour, reminding himself of home, for all these plants originated in China.

Chin often looked into his goldfish bowl, recalling how his father and his father's father before him had cultivated goldfish and bred them to achieve exotic varieties. Chin also looked out the window of his house into the park and saw the boys flying their kites—and they would remind him of the kite flights he had enjoyed as a boy back in China. In his house the brasses and bronzes and beautiful carvings all reminded Chin Fong Chow of home. Even the wallpaper on the wall was an invention from his native land, brought West by enterprising traders.

Much, much later in time, after the family had sent Chin Fong Chow's body back to the village a few miles from Canton for burial and he had long been laid to rest, the life of the young Chinese in America became considerably different.

By the 1930's Lu Yi, known as Fred Louie to his Western acquaintances, ran a popular Chinese restaurant in Portland, Oregon. Fred Louie served egg foo yong, chop suey, chow mein, fried rice, and various dishes that appealed to the Western palate. Fred Louie worshiped in the old way, and he set off firecrackers on the Chinese New Year and other important days, such as the Dragon Boat Festival day. However, Fred Louie's ambience was somewhat more American than Chin Fong Chow's had been. His wife was American-born, and his children were more American than he, so much so that they could hardly speak Chinese.

James Wong was an electrician in San Francisco. In 1950 he moved out of Chinatown and resettled over in Marin County. At first there were some raised eyebrows, but they were soon lowered. James Wong's wife, Mary, also born in Chinatown, grew up and went to school there during the bad old days, but Mary was a housewife in 1950. She shopped in the Safeway store for most of her groceries. The Wongs did not have a shrine in their house, but were as determinedly agnostic as any Caucasian in the neighborhood. They read with great interest any news they could get about mainland China, but were very careful not to say much about it in public, because the Americans around them did not understand what was happening in China. On Sundays they went back to Chinatown in their Chevrolet and shopped for *bok choy* and dried shrimp and Dzechuan pepper in the Chinese markets on Grant Avenue. They picked up a Chinese newspaper or two, most of them from Hong Kong and Taiwan. Occasionally, they found something from Peking or Shanghai, but not very often in those days of McCarthyism in America.

Another twenty years went by. Now the oldest son, Frank

Wong, is a student at Berkeley. He speaks hardly a word of Chinese. He wears blue jeans, an old work shirt, and love beads to class. He is trying to decide whether to be an architect or an engineer. He has the feeling that there is still a kind of discrimination in the workaday world, no matter what the laws say, but it does not come through on campus. Frank is middle-sized and outgoing, and on the telephone one would not know whether his name was Wong or Long.

Frank Wong will probably marry a Chinese-American girl, but then again he might not. A generation earlier he would have almost certainly done so, because of the similarity of backgrounds, the discrimination that still prevailed in the United States, and the enormous problem of breaking out of the Chinese community. In the 1970's, however, the breakout is easy. Almost nowhere do Orientals have difficulty in housing or employment. Colleges are looking for Oriental Americans to give them scholarships. The communications trades and professions are pleading with Oriental Americans to join their ranks. The doctor or other professional finds it a little easier to stick to the Chinese community, but the hospitals are totally unemotional about accepting his services.

Like the Chinese, the Japanese who came to America usually emigrated for economic reasons. In the very beginning some political refugees came to the West, but after that it was people looking for wealth. The grandfather of United States Senator Daniel K. Inouye of Hawaii was one. He came to Hawaii in the nineteenth century to make enough money to pay off a family debt. It took him thirty years, and by the time he had it paid, he had become acclimated to the islands and remained.

The Japanese were much more eager to be "assimilated" culturally into American society than the Chinese. The Japanese brought their own foods and tastes with them, but they were very adaptable. In his book *Nisei: The Quiet*

Americans, Bill Hosokawa tells the tale of Manyumon Fujita, who settled on a sharecrop farm in 1906 near Billings, Montana. Fujita settled in, cleared the land, uprooted the sagebrush, and built a farm. He grew beans and sugar beets. He wore shoes made from old canvas bean sacks. Every spring he had to auction off his farm implements to pay his debts. Then he bought more implements on credit and farmed a new crop. The Fujitas were the only Japanese family in the area. Most of the time they ate something they called *bottera,* a kind of pancake stuffed with sweet beans. When they went to town, a two-day trip, they headed for the first saloon, where Manyumon Fujita drank with his friends and the kids filled up on the free lunch. Their assimilation was almost complete.

Japanese men imported their wives from the homeland, usually by mail order. The girls came from their native villages. They were whisked off the boat, out of their kimonos, and into corsets, and informed that they must take on a new way of life.

The Japanese had their own stores, their own Buddhist temples, their own restaurants and hotels, which catered to Japanese tastes. They brought bamboo and wicker furniture to America. Although a great number of the Buddhists were converted to Christianity, particularly Methodism, Buddhist churches in America continued to be strong, and by 1968 there were fifty-seven churches in the association.

The Issei kept the old traditions. They made *tsukenomo* pickles and observed the old-country tradition of paying off their debts at the end of the year (if they could). They ate raw fish and soy sauce, black beans and seaweed, and they spoke to their children in Japanese.

The children ate peanut-butter sandwiches and hamburgers, went to the movies, and spoke to their families in English. The Issei brought judo to America. They held clan reunions on New Year's, where they served Japanese food and sake, the hot rice wine of the islands. As far as language was concerned, the Nisei tended to lose the mother tongue much more quickly than did the Chinese, although there were a number of Japanese-language schools, particularly in California. These schools taught Japanese and *Shushin,* or the Japanese moral code, which was basically Confucian.

Some followed the old marriage customs, in which families arranged the marriage. Charles Kamayatsu was one of these. His wife was selected by his family and the wedding was arranged by a *haishakunin,* or go-between. It was a very happy marriage.

Most Nisei did not seek to retain Japanese culture. They were encouraged by such eminent men as Prince Iyesato Tokugawa, president of the Japanese House of Peers, to "work hard and make yourselves such fine citizens of the United States that you will be liked, respected, and welcomed everywhere."

So the Japanese tended to accept American culture as much as they were allowed.

As for the other Orientals, the Koreans, the Indians, the Indonesians, the Annamese—since they came to America in smaller numbers, they tended to band together more tightly and to identify themselves with their own country. Yet Indian culture has offered the West not only religious experience and mysticism, but a literature of its own, and many other gifts, including the system of numbers Westerners call Arabic.

The cultural interchange has worked both ways. It is still working, and it has become apparent that the West has a great deal to learn from the East in matters of art, music, philosophy, and outlook on life.

Appendix

Basic Laws and Rules Governing the Immigration of Orientals into the United States

1. *The Burlingame Treaty of 1868.* This treaty recognized an "inalienable right" of men to migrate freely from one country to another. It particularly established mutual and reciprocal relationships between the United States and China.

2. *The Chinese Exclusion Act of 1882.* This law suspended the immigration of Chinese laborers for ten years. It excepted teachers and other professionals, merchants, and travelers. It denied Chinese the right of naturalization as American citizens. It was extended in 1892 and in 1904, the second time for an indefinite period. Thus it became the basic law under which Chinese immigration was stopped.

3. *The Scott Act of 1888.* This law prohibited the return to the United States of any Chinese laborers who had left the country.

4. *The Gentlemen's Agreements.* Beginning in 1907 the United States and Japan made agreements limiting the number of Japanese who could come to the United States. The agreements extended and changed slightly from time to time over the years. The result was to hamper Japanese immigration.

5. *The Immigration Act of 1924.* This law forbade Chinese women entrance into the United States for the purpose of residence. It was also used to exclude other Orientals, including the Japanese.

6. *Repeal of the Exclusion Acts, 1943.* This law, signed by President Roosevelt, gave the Chinese for the first time the rights of naturalization as American citizens. It established a quota of 105 Chinese immigrants per year.

7. *War Brides Act of 1945.* This law allowed wives of American servicemen to enter the United States more easily than others and outside the quota system. It enabled many Orientals to come to America.

8. *Displaced Persons Act of 1948.* This law enabled a number of Orientals to gain entry into the United States.

9. *Refugee Act of 1953.* This law brought in a number of refugees of the Chinese revolution.

10. *Presidential Directive of 1962.* This law took off restrictions on the entrance of Hong Kong refugees and let some fifteen thousand Chinese into the country.

11. *The Immigration Law of 1965.* This law abolished the old quota system of immigration, based on national origins. It established a quota of twenty thousand for each independent country outside the Western Hemisphere. This law has become the basic immigration doctrine of the United States.

Bibliography

Chinese

Barth, Gunther, *Bitter Strength: A History of the Chinese in the United States, 1850–1870,* Harvard University Press, Cambridge, Mass., 1964.

Chinese Immigration, California State Printing Office, 1876. A Report of a special legislative committee.

Nee, Victor G., and Brett DeBary, *Longtime Californ': A Documentary Study of an American Chinatown,* Pantheon Books, New York, 1973.

Japanese

Girdner, Audrie, and Anne Loftis, *The Great Betrayal, The Evacuation of the Japanese-Americans During World War II,* Macmillan, New York, 1969.

Hosokawa, Bill, *Nisei: The Quiet Americans.* Morrow, 1969.

McWilliams, Carey, *Prejudice: Japanese-Americans, Symbol of Racial Intolerance,* Little, Brown, Boston, 1944. Reprinted by The Shoe String Press, Hamden, Connecticut, 1971.

Indians

Adams, Heribert, *Modernizing Racial Domination: The Dynamics of South Africa Politics,* University of California Press, Berkeley, 1971.

Gandhi, Mohandas K., *Autobiography,* Heinman Press, New York, 1969. Paper ed. by Beacon Press, Boston, 1957.

Hopkinson, Tom, *South Africa,* Time-Life (Life World Library), New York, 1969.

Nanda, B. R., *M. Gandhi,* Allied Publishers, Bombay, 1958.

Niddrie, David L., *South Africa: Nation or Nations?* Van Nostrand-Reinhold, New York, 1968.

Hawaii

Kuykendall, Ralph S., and A. Grove Day, *Hawaii: A History,* Prentice-Hall, Englewood Cliffs, N.J., 1961.

Lind, Andrew W., *Hawaii's People,* University of Hawaii Press, Honolulu, 1970 (3d ed.).

General

Makers of America, 10 vols. Encyclopedia Britannica Educational Corporation, Chicago.

Index